THE LSP METHOD

THE LSP METHOD

How to

ENGAGE PEOPLE AND SPARK INSIGHTS USING THE LEGO® SERIOUS PLAY® METHOD

MICHAEL FEARNE

THE LSP METHOD
How to Engage People and Spark Insights
Using the LEGO® Serious Play® Method

ISBN 978-1-5445-1681-3 *Hardcover*
978-1-5445-1679-0 *Paperback*
978-1-5445-1680-6 *Ebook*

For Lily & Maya

CONTENTS

PART III. CUSTOMISE

LEGO® COPYRIGHT INFORMATION

Part 1

THE FOUNDATION

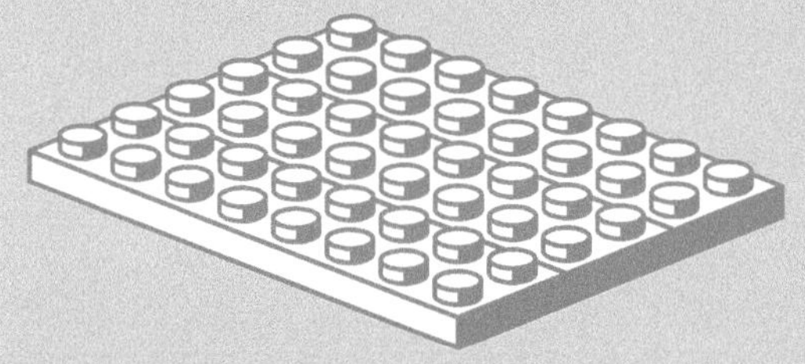

Chapter 1

INTRODUCTION

'Michael must be a drug dealer. He travels around the country and overseas with big bags of LEGO. He solves business problems with a kid's toy and gets paid for it. That's not a job. He must be a drug dealer.'

That was the conversation among my partner's five brothers when they found out what I do for a living. To them, what I did was so implausible. It made more sense that I was the kingpin of some international crime syndicate than a LEGO Serious Play facilitator.

I encounter that sort of scepticism all the time, from family members, clients and people sitting in the room at the start of one of my sessions. I get it. The premise of the LEGO® Serious Play® method sounds ridiculous: use a child's toy to tackle serious topics like strategy, innovation, collaboration and change.

It *is* ridiculous. But it works.

Thousands of LEGO Serious Play people, running thousands of LEGO Serious Play sessions around the world, prove this method works. But it's not enough for me to tell you that. You need to experience it for yourself.

That's what this book is all about. You get a chance to learn the method, experience it and test it out for yourself. Then you can decide if it becomes a tool you want to use to engage a group, explore a topic and get results.

1.1 THE SERIOUS SIDE OF LEGO

When I say LEGO Serious Play (LSP) to people, most of them get caught up on the 'LEGO' and the 'Play'. But the important word is that one in the middle: 'Serious'.

LEGO is just the medium, the tool you use. Play is simply one of many enablers the method uses. Both the LEGO and the Play serve the ultimate purpose of a Serious outcome.

But let's take a step back. Why would you even want to use LEGO in this serious way?

Have you ever been in a meeting or workshop and felt it was hard to get a word in? You had some good ideas, but the conversation was dominated by a few, and you left the meeting feeling that the outcome could have been better.

You had more to give.

On the flip side, have you ever run a meeting or workshop and felt like you weren't getting the best out of the people in the room? You knew they had the talent and the ideas, but it wasn't coming out in the conversation.

They had more to give.

What if there were a way to run our meetings, workshops and classes that allowed you and your people to give all they had? To feel engaged in the conversation and feel real ownership of the outcomes?

That's the promise of LEGO Serious Play.

Let's take a closer look at our current meetings and workshops and see how they are failing us. Imagine a typical business meeting where eight people get together to solve a business issue. Let's see what's going on under the surface that impacts the outcome:

- **The meeting is a talk fest.** One or two people are talking; everyone else is listening. Verbal and auditory? Yes. Visual? No. Kinaesthetic? No. Too bad if you prefer to engage with complex or new ideas by seeing them and touching them. For this meeting and most meetings, it's words all the way.
- **The meeting is for extroverts.** They feel comfortable speaking up. The introverts keep quiet.

- **The meeting is for analytical types.** The messiness of creativity gets pushed to the side.
- **The meeting is linear and sequential.** One idea is discussed at a time. One after the other. Park this, park that; we'll get to it later. It's hard to see connections when you talk about one thing at a time.
- **The meeting is for the powerful.** Those without power don't get heard.

Most meetings are skewed towards the extroverted, analytical, powerful types who like to talk. And they are the ones who dominate.

The rest of the group have a more difficult time. Those who prefer to visualise things, those who enjoy getting hands on, those who see the connections between ideas, the quieter ones, the creative types and those with less power are all forced to struggle through.

You know, most of the room. Sound familiar?

All that untapped potential is sitting there, along with the ideas and stories that could make all the difference. But people aren't engaged, and they aren't bringing all their talent to the table.

Quite simply, the format we use in meetings and workshops is failing us and the outcome is suffering.

1.2 'CHANGE THE PROCESS, CHANGE THE OUTCOME'

Johan Roos (coinventor of LEGO Serious Play) summed up LSP perfectly when he said, 'Change the process, change the outcome'. If you change the way a meeting is run, you can change the outcome you get from it.

Let's change the process by adding in LSP. We'll take the variables mentioned earlier and see what happens:

- **Power.** The LSP process levels the playing field, allowing everyone to be heard.
- **Creatives.** They finally have a medium where they can express their creativity.
- **Introverts.** The LSP process allows people to take turns and gives introverts a comfortable platform to express their ideas.
- **Connections.** In LSP sessions, the group can see multiple ideas at anytime, allowing novel connections to be made.
- **Verbal/Auditory.** There's still lots of talking and listening, but it's more evenly distributed.
- **Visual.** Everyone can see the conversation in physical form.
- **Kinaesthetic.** People are using their hands to build the conversation and build the solution.

By incorporating LSP, we've gone from a meeting where only the extroverted, analytical, powerful over-talkers dominate to one where everyone is engaged and is contributing through multiple dimensions. The ideas, the conversations and the solutions that flow are better for it. And isn't that why we gather together in the first place? The goal should be to use all the talent in the room to come up with the best outcome.

This picture is not confined to the world of work. These same factors occur whenever we get together in groups, and they limit the outcome. It's clear that the way we gather is holding us back. LEGO Serious Play changes that by unlocking all the experiences and ideas that are there within every single person.

1.3 LSP IN ACTION

You might be thinking, 'Yes, but what does that sort of meeting *look* like'?

Here it is in picture form:

1. You put a pile of special LEGO in front of people and ask them a question on the topic you want to discuss.
2. Individuals build their answer to that question as a LEGO model, using metaphor and storytelling

1

2

techniques. The key is that participants build the intangible ideas, concepts and experiences floating around in their mind, giving them form in LEGO. LSP is not about building literal things like cars or prototypes. The person in picture 2 is building the opportunities and challenges facing a particular company. Throughout the book, you'll see more examples of what people build.

3. People take turns to share the story of their model (their answer to the initial question).

4. People listen.
5. Sometimes it's funny.

6A

6. Often it's serious.

6B

7A

7. A lot of individual reflections and insights are shared.

7B

8A

8. Sometimes people build group models.

8B

9. And this results in group reflection and insights.

10. The end result is better conversations. And better outcomes.

The photo on the following page shows a series of actions a team developed from an LSP workshop.

1.4 WHAT THIS BOOK WILL TEACH YOU

In this book, you'll learn everything you need to know in order to run meetings, workshops and classes using the LEGO Serious Play method.

You'll learn:

- The history of LSP and what a typical session looks like (chapter 2)
- The stories of people just like you who learnt LSP and are now using it (chapter 3)

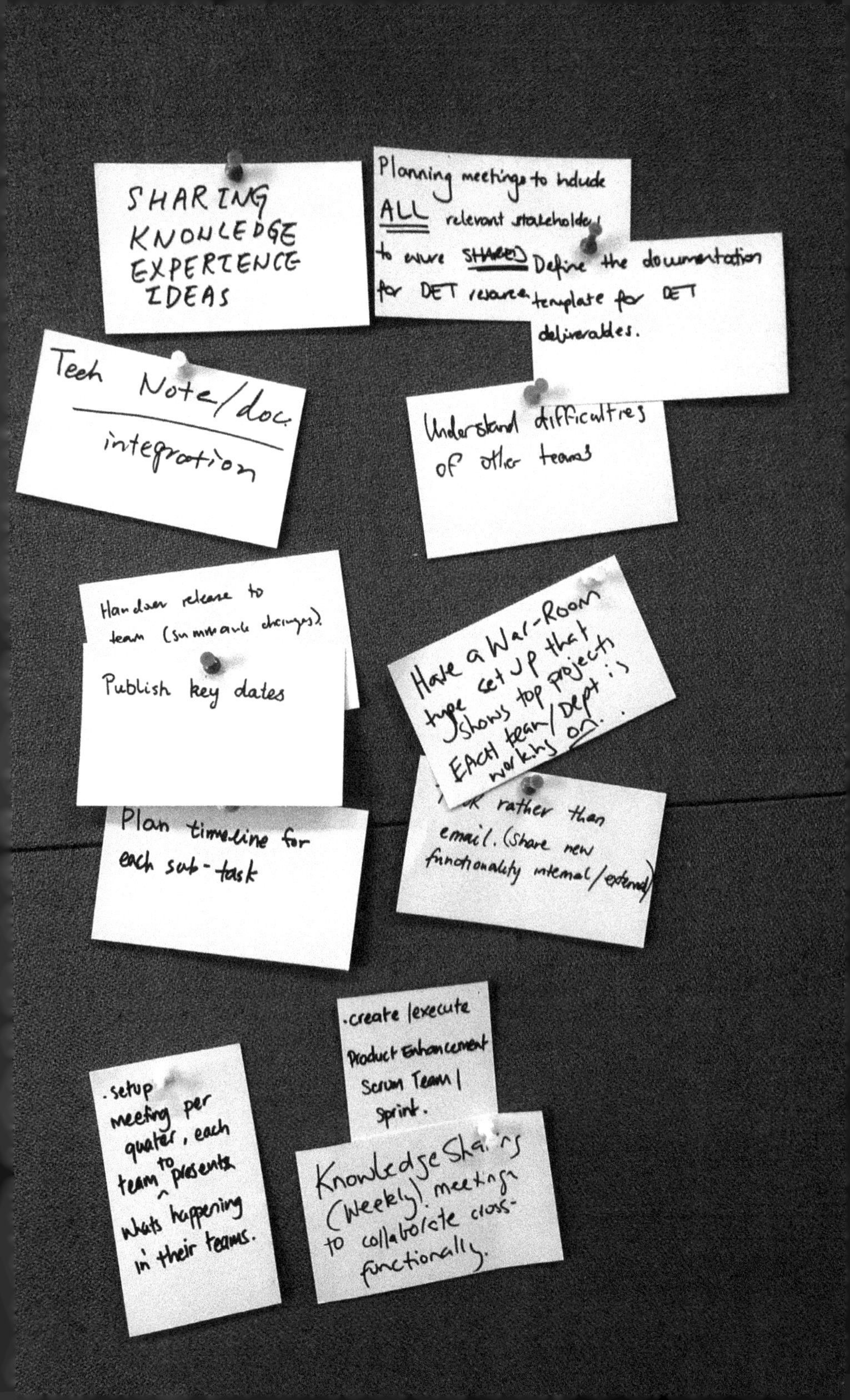

SHARING
KNOWLEDGE
EXPERIENCE
IDEAS

Planning meetings to include ALL relevant stakeholders to ensure SHARED for DET resource.

Define the documentation template for DET deliverables.

Tech Note/doc integration

Understand difficulties of other teams

Handover release to team (summarise changes).

Publish key dates

Have a War-Room type set up that shows top projects EACH team/Dept is working on.

... rather than email. (Share new functionality internal/external)

Plan timeline for each sub-task

. create/execute Product Enhancement Scrum Team/Sprint.

. setup meeting per quarter, each team to present whats happening in their teams.

Knowledge Sharing (Weekly) meetings to collaborate cross-functionally.

- How to set up your sessions, including which LEGO to use (chapter 4)
- The best introduction to use for your sessions (chapter 5)
- The warm-up activity that never fails to get people ready (chapter 6)
- Key activities: Individual Models (chapter 7), Shared Models (chapter 8), Landscape Models (chapter 9), other activities (chapter 10)
- Options for the final activity, used to end the session and make an impact (chapter 11)
- How to design your own sessions (chapter 12)
- Outlines of example sessions (chapter 13)
- The science behind the LSP method (chapter 14)
- How to talk with people so they want to do LSP, an overview of some trademark guidelines, how to do LSP online and how you can take your LSP learning further (chapter 15)

1.5 WHY LISTEN TO ME?

So why listen to me? Because I'm good at what I do, and I'll teach you what I know.

It took me months to decide whether or not I should put that line in the book. I'm not one to blow my own trumpet. But it's the truth, and here is why:

TOP: Me facilitating an LSP session for fifty people in late 2019. BOTTOM: Same session. I'm at a table, enthralled, as one of the participants shares the story of their model. That's why I love LSP: for the stories. Getting drawn into someone else's world and seeing their point of view, their insights, is magic.

The strategies and techniques described in this book are based on my experiences of facilitating groups since 2006 and using LSP full time since 2013.

After studying psychology at university, I started my career at the management consulting firm KPMG. There, I learnt the foundations of group dynamics and how to run a workshop.

I left KPMG to work directly with some of the largest organisations in Australia and around the world, helping teams have better conversations. In the early days, I didn't use LSP. I used a wide range of tools. Then, in 2013, I experienced what LEGO Serious Play could do and have been doing it ever since. It's all I do now.

My clients include Ernst & Young, KPMG, Google, Lexus, government departments, telecommunications giants, global IT consultancies and big financial institutions, as well as small organisations: startups, digital agencies and nonprofits.

My work has extended to training other people in LSP so they can run their own sessions. People at Ernst & Young, KPMG, Daimler, the defence industry, digital agencies and universities, as well as coaches and consultants. I have even taught people in the innovation lab at the LEGO Group itself.

I have run hundreds of LSP sessions, taking thousands of people through the method. I have trained and certified hundreds of people in the LSP method to go out and make their own impact.

This book you hold is seven years of my life. Over twenty thousand hours of practice and thought are distilled down into a set of steps, tips and insights ready for you to learn from and implement.

I have a somewhat unhealthy obsession with this method. I fall asleep thinking about it and wake up wanting to use it.

Am I too invested in LSP? Possibly. I'll let you judge that as we go through the book. But by being this obsessive about LSP, I've fast-tracked my thinking and my experience, and you get the benefits of that.

Why would I spend so much time obsessing over this?

It's not the LEGO. If it weren't for LSP and what it does, I wouldn't really touch any LEGO. For me, it's the beautiful blend of getting people thinking differently, the stories they tell and the insights they come up with. I love setting the stage and providing a platform for people to be engaged, tell authentic stories and have those aha moments—and, as a bonus, get real business outcomes from that process. That's a match made in my sort of heaven.

When I saw what LSP could do, I realised everyone needed to be doing it. All the decisions I've made since

2013 have been aimed at getting LSP into other people's hands and showing them how to do it. From teaching the method in person, to developing an online course, to building a community of practice, all the way through to this book, it's been about increasing access to the best LSP knowledge.

My vision is for LSP to be as ubiquitous as a Post-it note or whiteboard. It will be there in every meeting room; everyone will know how to do it (and when to do it). It will be another tool we all have to achieve better engagement and better outcomes.

1.6 WHAT THIS BOOK IS AND WHAT IT ISN'T

PRACTICAL

This is a practical guide, not a definitive bible.

There are a lot of different ways to do LSP. People have taken the base LSP method and layered on other techniques. In some cases, they've improved it in niche areas, but in other cases, they've complicated it unnecessarily.

This book is all the good stuff: the core of what you need. I've done the work of sifting through what's useful and what's not and taking the complex and making it simple. I could have written a 500-page manual. LSP can be that complex. But that's not practical or useful to you. This book will be.

PRACTISE

LSP is a hands-on method. To fully understand it, you need to do it. This book gives you the start you need. But practise what you read here. Practise with family, with friends, with trusted colleagues and with other LSP people.

Don't do it alone. Get a friend to read this book and learn LSP with you. Often, when you want to run LSP with your team, you should be part of the group participating, not the facilitator. Having a friend who knows the method and can run a session for you is invaluable.

FACILITATION SKILLS

You don't need to be a professional facilitator to run sessions using LSP. But you do need some facilitation skills or the ability to manage a group during a session. Building up your facilitation skills will help you get more out of the LSP method.

FIND YOUR METHOD IN THE METHOD

The way I've written this book is very prescriptive: 'Do this step, then do this step'. But view this book as a baseline, a foundation for you to start with. If, after a couple of sessions, you want to run it differently, go for it! I encourage you to 'Find your method in the method'.

Make sure to keep an eye on the results, however. The LSP method is a delicate dance, and you might experience some unintended consequences, even when you make only minor changes. If you need a reset, return to this book as a baseline.

THE WORLD OF WORK

LSP works in many different contexts: work, education, community, therapy, family and anytime we gather in groups to talk.

I have trained people to use LSP in all those other areas. But my world is the world of work. The examples I'll use in this book are from my own sessions.

1.7 ACKNOWLEDGMENTS

Lastly, I would like to acknowledge the previous work done by many people to get LEGO Serious Play to where it is today. I didn't invent LEGO Serious Play. I learnt the base method from others just like you're about to. I've used these activities over hundreds of workshops. I've changed them in parts, added to them, taken away from them and made them easier to apply and learn. But this is all built upon the great work that many people have done over the last two decades. And so, to everyone who has contributed to the development of LEGO Serious Play, I thank you.

Let's get to it. The first place to start is way back at the beginning of LEGO Serious Play.

Chapter 2

THE WORLD OF LEGO SERIOUS PLAY

It's the late 1990s.

The LEGO Group has been around for sixty-five years, making children's toys. It's a huge, iconic company that has helped enrich the lives of many children through play and imagination.

But the late 1990s is not a good time for the Danish toymaker. Profits are down and threats are on the horizon.

Two business professors, Johan Roos and Bart Victor, are working with the LEGO Group on a leadership management program. They sit down with the CEO of the LEGO Group, Kjeld Kirk Kristiansen, and discuss how poor the strategy-making process is in the corporate world. Too many boxes being ticked and not enough original thought. Through these conversations, LEGO

Serious Play was born as a better way to do corporate strategy.

The method has since evolved beyond strategy and beyond the LEGO Group, but that's where it all started.

The next phase of LSP's development took place between 2000 and 2010. Through research and experimentation, several teams working for the LEGO Group turned this initial idea into a sound methodology.

In 2010, the LEGO Group decided to open source LSP and release it to the world.

From 2010 to 2020, the method grew rapidly. There are now two-, three- and four-day courses, run by the community, that people can attend to master the method. An online course, yearly conferences and communities of practise are all pushing the LSP method forward.

The future of the method looks bright.

2.1 DEFINING LEGO SERIOUS PLAY

Now we know where the method came from. Let's wrap our heads around what it is.

One of the challenges of LSP is describing it to people because it can be so many things.

On one level, it's easy. In an LSP session, you ask questions and people answer them by building a LEGO model using metaphors and story. From that, people have better conversations and gain deeper insights. But that definition only describes the process of how you do it.

You could focus on the types of sessions and the outcomes you get: for instance, LSP as a strategy tool, a team dynamics tool or a change management tool. But even that only describes individual use cases.

Ever since I started using LSP, I've been searching for a definition that encompasses all that the method can do. I've come across some fantastic definitions from leading facilitators.

Sebastian Simand describes LSP as a 'kinetic, metaphorical communication and idea stimulation tool'.

Another interesting description is from Sean Blair:

- Does it use LEGO bricks? Yes.
- Does it involve play? Yes.
- Is it facilitated by a skilled LSP facilitator? Yes.
- Do people use metaphors and storytelling? Yes.
- Does it follow a process? Yes.
- Does it follow the LSP etiquette? Yes.

If it does all these things, then it's LEGO Serious Play.

A third description comes from Phil Culhane: 'In our work, LSP is a means, not an end. It is a 3-D conceptual modelling tool that enables high participation rates and enables trust to emerge'.

What I love about Sebastian, Sean and Phil's descriptions is how expansive they are. If you follow a few core elements, then LSP is much more flexible than just a strategy tool.

For me, LSP comes down to a simple truth: LEGO Serious Play is a different way to think and a different way to have a conversation.

The 'different way' bit is where all the detail is. LSP uses some physical tools and some steps to change the way we think and the way we communicate. The end result is that we look at a topic or issue differently, we have different conversations about it and come up with different insights.

The strategy use of LSP is just one type of thinking/conversation it's good for.

The change management use of LSP is just one type of thinking/conversation it's good for.

In my work, I see LSP used in project management, marketing, IT, customer experience, risk management, higher education, psychology, community consultation, change management and many other conversations around the world.

When you realise that LEGO Serious Play is simply a different way to think and have a conversation, the number of potential uses is mind-blowing.

2.2 WHO USES LSP?

Lots of organisations are using and have used LSP: big and small, private and government, business and education. It is used around the world in Europe, the US, South America and Asia. I could reel off a long list of companies, a who's who of industry.

Since 2013, I have worked with the likes of KPMG, Ernst & Young, Google and the LEGO Group itself as well as a whole host of small and medium businesses you have never heard of.

Having said all that, I don't know of any large company that uses LSP across their entire organisation. LSP is still seen as an innovative, 'cutting edge' method. It's used by innovators in an organisation—those who are pushing the boundaries to seek better results. The reason for this is right there in the core idea of LSP: bringing a child's toy to work.

Organisations as a whole system struggle to get past this superficial understanding. But those innovators who do, reap the rewards.

Consider the adoption curve. We're in the early adopter stage with LSP. As more people get exposed to LSP and get comfortable with it, it will spread more broadly in organisations.

Currently, the work I do with LSP focuses on change management, team culture and innovation because of my background in those areas.

However, I've taught the LSP method to people who are using it to:

- Change the way teams collaborate in the defence industry
- Engage people in the topic of risk management
- Enhance their customer experience workshops
- Consult with communities in Australia and the indigenous population of East Timor
- Coach individuals on career and personal branding
- Innovate in the product management field
- Help school principals envision strategies for a new future
- Teach students in university everything from marketing to IT to English literature
- Help people plan for retirement

And in hundreds of other ways.

In the next chapter, you're going to hear more from other people out in the field who are using LEGO Serious Play.

2.3 TYPICAL LSP SESSION

LSP is a very flexible tool, in both what it's used for and the format it takes.

If someone asked me to describe the ideal LSP session it would be:

- Six people plus one facilitator
- Three and a half hours
- Focused on an issue where participants need to
  (1) understand the current state,
  (2) envision a future state and
  (3) identify the actions needed to bridge the gap

But you can vary each of those dimensions (numbers, time commitment and format).

LSP NUMBERS

LSP can work with any number. You can run it one-on-one in a coaching session. You can scale it up to hundreds of people (I've run a session with 120). I personally prefer the smaller sessions, under ten people. In that environment, I feel I can add more as a facilitator. But the method works with any number of people.

LSP TIME COMMITMENT

With a first-time group, you need at least two hours. Once people know the method you can run sessions in as little as an hour and a half.

At the other end, LSP can take two days! That was the length of the original LSP strategy session that was devised back in the early 2000s, although in my experience, there aren't a lot of opportunities to do a two-day LSP session.

Most of my LSP sessions are in the two- to four-hour range. Given that this is the practical guide to LEGO Serious Play, we're going to focus on sessions in that timeframe.

LSP FORMAT

All LSP sessions run according to this format:

- **Skills Building**. You, as the facilitator, get the group to do a warm-up activity called Skills Building. This activity varies depending on whether the group are new to LSP or already familiar with the method. A description of the activities and how to run them is covered in chapters 5 and 6.

- **LSP Activities**. You take the group through a combination of the LEGO Serious Play activities outlined in chapters 7 through 10. Along the way, the group have interesting conversations and capture new insights.

- **Final Activity**. The session finishes with a final activity to help crystallise the new insights gathered and to decide on what actions to take. There are lots of options here, some of which are detailed in chapter 11.

EXAMPLE

Here is a high-level example of an LSP session in practice:

Back in 2014, I ran a session for Australia Post (the national mail service in Australia). The group was a newly formed recruitment team. The objectives were for everyone to know (1) each other's role, (2) where they fit into the team and (3) what they wanted their team culture to be.

There were twelve participants, and I had three hours for the workshop.

After the introduction, I took them through the set LSP Skills Building. Once they were familiar with the method, I got them to build Individual Models around their strengths and roles. They shared their models and stories with the group.

We then moved on to their team culture, building individually at first, then as a group and establishing a shared vision of what they wanted to achieve. We finished off by developing concrete actions the group could take away to achieve that vision.

Skills Building -> LSP activities -> final activity

2.4 THE IMPORTANCE OF METAPHOR AND STORYTELLING

You've read about what a typical session is in terms of numbers, time and format. But there is one more key element that I want to introduce you to.

LSP works best when people build using metaphors and storytelling.

When most people think about LEGO, they think of building literal, real objects from the outside world: 'I'll represent this object I can see, in LEGO form'. Models become mini, stylised LEGO versions of the real world.

If people end up building in this very literal way in your LSP session, then the method loses a lot of its power. Using metaphors and stories drives new insights, and that is what gives LSP its power.

What does it mean to build using metaphor and storytelling?

Throughout this book, you'll see lots of examples of different metaphorical LSP builds. In chapter 6, you'll learn the exact steps to deliver at the start of an LSP session to make sure your participants build using metaphor and storytelling.

As a quick example, take the case of a simple bit of spiky LEGO grass. It could be just grass, or you could place it in your model and have it be an obvious metaphor for environment or sustainability.

But what if we put that grass on top of a Minifigure's head? Suddenly that grass becomes an explosion of ideas, innovation, creativity.

Instead of the grass being on top, maybe the grass is underneath the Minifigure. Except it's not grass; it's a spiky situation, and this a metaphor for a problem this person is facing.

What if the grass is facing outwards, and now, it represents this person's style of communication: blasting out orders while not listening to those around them.

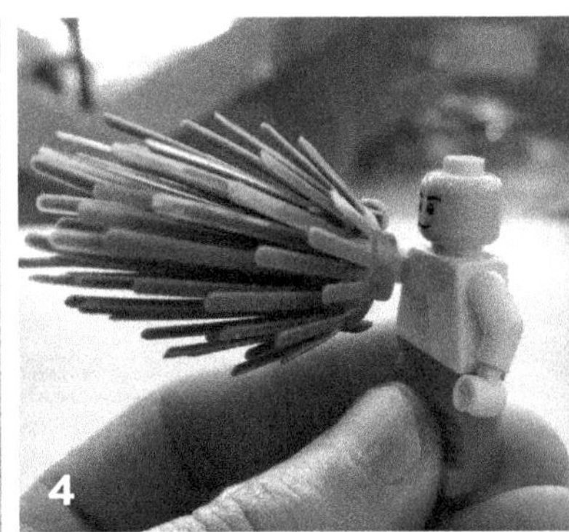

1. Environment? Sustainability? 2. Innovation? Creativity?
3. A challenge? 4. Communication style?

One simple bit of grass has variously represented environment, sustainability, ideas, innovation, creativity, a problem and a person's style of communication. Each one of those uses has a metaphor associated with it and invites us to view that situation in a different way.

And that's just one LEGO piece. Now imagine a small model with one hundred pieces, some of which have been assigned metaphors by the builder. You start to get an idea of the rich worlds you can create.

The overall message here is that the bricks can be whatever you want them to be. Whatever meaning you want to give them will help you to build interesting models with captivating stories, and that will change the way you think and communicate.

You'll see more examples from chapter 6 onwards. But as you're going through the book, learning the method, always have this concept of metaphor and story in the back of your mind. My best LSP sessions have happened when the group took this 'build in metaphor' concept and ran wild with it.

2.5 THE BEST WAY TO LEARN LSP

Over my years of teaching LSP to many people, I've found the best sequence for learning the method is:

1. Learn how to facilitate the separate activities (Individual, Shared, Landscape and others)
2. Learn how to put them together and design any LSP session
3. Apply that knowledge to design a customised session that fits your objective

This book follows that sequence. It ensures you have a solid foundation in delivering the method and designing sessions for whatever need you have in the future.

But before we start learning the method, I want to take a short detour so you can meet some other people who have learnt LSP and are now using it to change their work.

Chapter 3

PEOPLE USING LSP

In this chapter, you'll hear from people who were just like you: curious about LSP and how it could help them. They learned the method and are now using LEGO Serious Play out in the world.

I share their stories because it's easy to talk about LEGO Serious Play in the abstract, but it's important to always come back to how real people are using it to make real change happen.

ELMA PANGILINAN

Talent Development

Ernst & Young, Singapore

What do you use LSP for?

I use LSP for team planning sessions, future state role-mapping and conversations on becoming a trusted business advisor. I've also had the chance to run an

LSP workshop for young leaders who are inheriting their family businesses. LSP helps them identify their strengths and define the future that they envision for their respective businesses.

What's the Best Outcome You've Seen When Using LSP?

A team whose members hardly spoke to each other started communicating better. Some of them didn't feel comfortable expressing themselves in words, so they used the bricks to translate what was on their minds into something very concrete and relatable. They felt heard and valued. That's fulfilling for any facilitator and very useful for a leader who is seeking new ideas from their team.

ANDERS MØLLER & BJÖRN BEHN

Managing Partner and Global Innovation Lead

Diplomatic Rebels, Denmark

What do you use LSP for?

LSP has proven to be a very powerful tool for our people-centred approach. It turns traditionally challenging conversations into engaging and playful experiences. Among our specific applications, you will find competency mapping, stakeholder management, value alignment and career planning.

What's the best outcome you've seen when using LSP?

One of our clients was reorganising their digital team around a new project requiring different competencies. To gauge the skills and motivations of the team members, we developed a two-by-two matrix mapping out the central aspects of the team's work.

Instead of a normal meeting, we got the participants to build their own skills and motivations using LEGO Serious Play. They then added these models to the two-by-two matrix landscape. Not only did they reflect upon their roles, but a rich discussion flourished on how they wanted to develop their competencies into the future.

AARON DAVIS

Academic Researcher and Project Facilitator
University of South Australia, Australia

What do you use LSP for?

I use LEGO Serious Play to help facilitate difficult discussions in my project work. It's great at breaking down power hierarchies. I also use it for personal thinking and reflection.

What's the best outcome you've seen when using LSP?

I was working with an organisation that was looking for some strategic direction. They were in the fortunate position of having significant financial resources, but they were not sure where they should be heading.

The founder and director of the organisation was a very senior figure in his field and was reluctant to engage when he saw the LEGO on the table. But after the warm-up exercise, he really began to embrace it. The LEGO was able to break down what was a significant power hierarchy within the board and allowed the participants the freedom to talk frankly.

Despite not quite getting complete agreement by the end of the session, there was noticeably more understanding of the various board members' strengths, ambitions and positions on some key issues.

By the end of the session, the director thanked me for 'the best strategy day he had ever been a part of' and was planning how he could introduce this into more of his work.

PHIL CULHANE

Strategic Change Advisor
CT Labs, Canada

What do you use LSP for?

Our consultancy is focused on providing transformative solutions to intractable, complex, systemic challenges. At certain points in the process, we need to bring groups together into an open space to engage in dialogue. Sometimes that dialogue is focused on discovery, sometimes on planning and sometimes on buy-in and commitment. For us, LSP is one of the tools in our Pandora's box.

What's the best outcome you've seen when using LSP?

We led a national action plan for persons with disabilities and had seventy-five participants with a full range of abilities/disabilities: persons without sight; persons who couldn't hear or couldn't speak; persons who had Multiple Sclerosis, Muscular Dystrophy and a range of other motor challenges; and persons with a range of mental health challenges. A full spectrum of potential challenges.

We asked them to do the entire three-day workshop using LSP. There was no difference between this highly varied group and any other group that we have ever worked with while using LSP. None of the disabilities provided any challenge to the use of LSP to perform the work at hand. In fact, I would say that LSP profoundly enabled the work.

I knew something very special was happening when I passed one table and listened in as a sixty-year-old man who had been without sight since birth showed his highly detailed model to his five table mates and said, 'If you look very closely, what you will see is...'.

JACQUELINE JACOB

Agile Practice Lead

Cognizant, Australia

What do you use LSP for?

We use LSP when teams are starting a new project. They need to uncover the skills they each bring to the team and work out how they will all come together towards a common goal.

We also use it at the end of projects when teams are planning out their next piece of work and are looking strategically at what their next move is. I find that LSP provides a good platform for a bigger discussion.

What's the best outcome you've seen?

The best outcome I have seen has been a workshop with a new team who didn't know one another and whose roles were unclear. We started by building models around skills and what they brought to the project and then moved onto a shared model, which led into a discussion about work practices and roles.

By the end of the workshop, people were having meaningful open discussions. I followed up with them a few weeks later and they were a happy, cohesive team.

GABU LOPEZ

Business and Performance Coach

Argentina

What do you use LSP for?

I use it for two different clients: companies and individuals.

In companies, I use it with teams. The main application areas are cultural transformation, branding, goal setting, strategy, scrum retrospectives, purpose/vision/mission and innovation and creativity, among other topics.

For individuals, I use LSP as a tool in my coaching practice. I work with executives who want to improve their performance and with people who want to reinvent their careers and make the transition for a purpose-driven job.

What's the best outcome you've seen when using LSP?

Everybody gets involved, even the more sceptical individuals. Usually, those who are the most uncomfortable at the beginning of the workshop are the most thankful and committed at the end.

LSP is a great tool for opening and maintaining difficult conversations because the emotional factor is usually put aside. When people get together and share their concerns in a nonjudgmental manner, they arrive at powerful conclusions and commit to a shared vision that they build together.

The insights are very profound. People open up when they can externalise what they are thinking. And by seeing a mock-up of their ideas in front of them, they access information they did not know they knew.

ELSKE VAN DE FLIERT

Academic

University of Queensland, Australia

But my research and consultancy work over the past decade has taken place in Indonesia, Vietnam, Timor Leste, Mongolia, China and East Africa.

What do you use LSP for?

I am an academic at the University of Queensland, where I teach and do research in the field of communication for social change. My research projects mostly relate to rural and agricultural development in the Global South. I work with rural communities (farmers, nomadic herders), local government, NGOs and researchers from many different disciplines.

The most exciting use of LSP in my work has been in relation to my research projects with partners and participants in Indonesia and Timor Leste. LSP has served to help local community members conceptualise desired change processes (e.g., post-disaster livelihood rehabilitation in an area affected by earthquakes). It has helped guide the direction of research for development initiatives. It was also used to support local partners in identifying their role in these projects and developing follow-up work plans.

In addition, I am using LSP in my teaching and PhD student supervision. I employ LSP to help students design and conceptualise their research projects.

What's the best outcome you've seen when using LSP?

The best outcome I have seen when using LSP is when people suddenly understand their own situation much better. They are able to articulate what they are doing and why they do what they do.

As such, LSP is a powerful tool for conscientisation, which is a major first step before people can identify what level and direction of change is desirable and possible and then effectively engage in making that change happen for themselves. I have seen this process of conscientisation occur with LSP in diverse groups of participants, from illiterate farmers in the Global South to academics with PhDs in Australian universities.

BEN MIZEN

Director and Lead Facilitator
Ideas Alchemy, United Kingdom

What do you use LSP for?

The majority of work that I use the LSP method for is in the area of developing teams. Whether it is assisting in their growth, discovering and working through dysfunctions, generating creative ideas, solving problems or formulating strategic plans, the safe boundaries of the process and etiquette of LSP create a safe space for learning. The shared dialogue and team ownership that flow from effective talking and listening are what clients really value.

I also use LSP for reflective practice with university students, conference creativity and managers who need to think differently on leadership issues.

What's the best outcome you've seen when using LSP?

Working with a large housing association on how to improve some of their processes. The workshop engaged multiple teams and stakeholders in building their functions and then collaboratively modelling the key processes. Alongside this, Agents that impact the process were built and connected to the process model. We then played a number of scenarios through the system.

The major outcomes were focused around simplifying unnecessary complexity, improving the sense of team and working on simpler communications.

GUY STEPHENS

Facilitator

United Kingdom

What do you use LSP for?

Strategy, vision setting, team alignment and personal development.

What's the best outcome you've seen when using LSP?

I was running a workshop for a team to help them come up with a different way to think about a problem they had struggled with for many months. They had looked at this problem from a variety of different angles but had not been able to make a breakthrough.

As you would expect, there were a range of personalities taking part in the workshop. This particular workshop was memorable for me, not because of the outcome, but because of one particular person who was so engaged and absorbed in the whole experience. He told really thoughtful stories about his models, shared openly and confidently and was obviously really enjoying the experience and the opportunity to play and explore.

When I reported back to the sponsor after the workshop, he was amazed. The sponsor said he would not have picked this particular person to be so engaged. This person typically would keep in the background, not step forward and not naturally engage.

When I asked this person about his experience, he said that there was something about the LEGO bricks that allowed him to connect and feel safe, and it was as if something was awakened in him.

Sometimes we need to remember to look in the unexpected or overlooked places for the real benefits of an LSP workshop!

LSP OUTCOMES

Elma, Anders, Bjorn, Aaron, Phil, Jacky, Gabu, Elske, Ben and Guy learnt the LSP method and now have a powerful new tool in their toolkit.

As we go through the book, they'll pop back in to share their best tips on LEGO Serious Play.

Part II

THE LSP SESSION

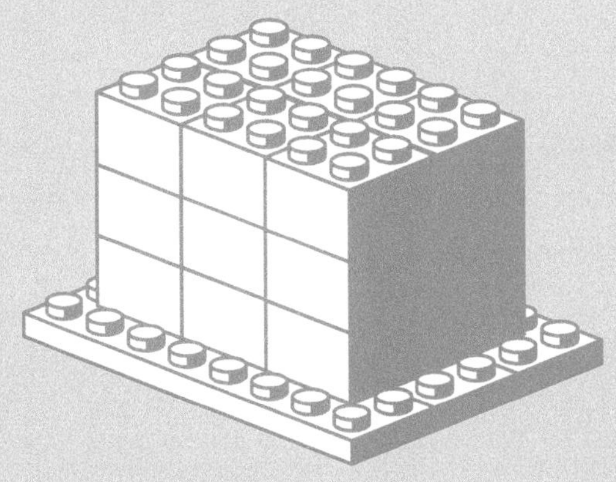

Chapters 4 through 12 show you all the steps that you, as facilitator, will need to follow to deliver your own LSP sessions. On the page below are the highlights of each chapter. They might not mean much to you now, but they show you the overall framework we will go through. At any point, you can come back to this page to see where you are in the bigger picture.

This page is replicated in appendix 3, where I also include one-page summaries for each chapter.

CHAPTER 4: PRE-SESSION

- Is LSP the right tool?
- Design the session
- Set up the room

CHAPTER 5: SESSION INTRODUCTION

- What is LSP?
- Who uses LSP and why?
- Six bricks activity
- Why LSP is different from LEGO
- Objective of the session

CHAPTER 6: SKILLS BUILDING

- Define the four steps (Question, Build, Share, Capture)
- Share the two tips (including examples)
- 'Build a tower with you in it' activity
- Explain This! activity (for groups that have already done the tower)

CHAPTER 7: INDIVIDUAL MODELS

- Individuals build LEGO models as answers to a question
- Your role as facilitator in each step

CHAPTER 8: SHARED MODELS

- A group combine Individual Models into one Shared Model
- Your role as facilitator in each step

CHAPTER 9: LANDSCAPE MODELS

- A group keep their Individual Models intact and place them in the Landscape to show relationships
- Your role as facilitator in each step

CHAPTER 10:OTHER ACTIVITIES

- Shared + Landscape (including Agents)

- Connections
- Non-LEGO activities

CHAPTER 11: FINAL ACTIVITY

- What do you normally do?
- Finish with actions: ORID
- Finish with something tangible: LEGO model or Kanban board

CHAPTER 12: DESIGN

- Find your key questions
- Draft the session outline
- Refine the questions
- Where to use the power of LSP

Chapter 4

PRE-SESSION

Before a LEGO Serious Play session there are three things you, as the facilitator, need to do:

- Decide if LSP is the right tool
- Design the session
- Set up the room

4.1 IS LSP THE RIGHT TOOL?

LSP works well when:

- The topic is complex
- There is no one right answer
- You want everyone's input and engagement

Here are some specific examples from the world of work:

- **Strategy**. The original use case. LSP can be used as part of the strategy-making and refining process.
- **Team Identity**. When a new team come together, LSP can be used to establish roles, culture and a vision for the team. It also works well for established teams who want to develop strategies to become high-performing teams.
- **Innovation**. LSP can be used as one part of an innovation process, providing a different lens to open up new insights and approaches.
- **Culture**. LSP can help with many aspects here, from diagnosing poor work cultures to establishing culture principles at the team or company level.
- **Change Management**. LSP helps individuals and teams understand current states and how to move to desired future states.
- **Team Collaboration**. LSP can give teams a framework for better collaboration within the team and between teams.
- **Design Thinking**. LSP can be integrated into other tools like design thinking. It works particularly well early in the design thinking process at the empathy stage as another way to dive deeper into the current situation.

- **Job Interviews.** LSP works well as a group interview activity and also in one-on-one interviews. It allows the interviewer to get past the typical, prepared answers and see the real person.
- **Coaching**. LSP can help a coachee to visualise their current issue, goals and a path forward.
- **Project Kick-Off Meetings**. LSP can help the project team set and manage expectations internally as well as with stakeholders.
- **Retrospectives.** Both regular fortnightly review meetings and end-of-project review meetings can be enhanced with LSP.
- **Customer Experience.** LSP can be combined with other tools to improve customer experience projects.

This is only a handful of the many ways you can use LSP. As you go through the book, you'll get a better feel for how it can be used in your world. We'll also return to this topic in chapter 12 when we talk about designing your own sessions.

> LSP is an amazing tool, but it's not always the answer.
>
> —Aaron Davis

4.2 WHEN *NOT* TO USE LSP

Here are a couple of areas where I've learned to *not* use LSP:

- **Simple Topic.** If you're dealing with a really simple topic or issue, ask yourself if spending the extra time that LSP takes is worth it.
- **One Right Answer.** If there is only one right answer to the topic or issue, there are often better analytical tools than LSP to uncover that one right answer.
- **Keeping Control.** If you don't want to hand over decision-making power to the group, engage everyone and get their commitment, then don't use LSP.
- **Training a Specific Skill.** LSP is not the best option if your objective is to teach people about communication or creativity using a LEGO activity. LSP is a generative method, which means that you, as facilitator, bring the questions, and the group generate the answers. LSP is not about teaching a specific skill like communication using LEGO.
- **I've Got the Answer.** Similarly, when you already have the answer and just want the group to 'get

it', LSP as a method is not about transmitting knowledge. It hands power over to the group and allows them to decide. They generate the answers.

- **Prototyping**. You can use LEGO to literally prototype something. But not LEGO Serious Play. It's a metaphorical tool that works at the level of ideas, experiences, opinions and concepts rather than on working physical prototypes.
- **Very Dysfunctional Teams**. LSP opens up communication. If a culture is very toxic, you might not want to open people up. This aspect is a matter of degrees. You can use LSP to help dysfunctional teams, but you need to be very cautious and use LSP as one of a number of interventions to help the group go from 'floundering' to 'functioning'.
- **Fun Team-Building Activity**. There are better activities for team building and pure fun. LSP needs an objective. The 'team-building' elements of LSP are built in. You get them for free while you're working towards a real objective. Using LSP as pure fun diminishes its power, so I always suggest other activities when someone wants just team building'.

4.3 DESIGN THE SESSION

Once you've decided to use LSP, you'd normally sit down to design a session. But you haven't learned the method yet!

We'll discuss design in much more detail when we get to chapter 12. But here are some simple prompts that will help you get ready for a session:

- **Why?** Get clear on your objective.
- **When?** The morning is best. Not straight after lunch.
- **Where?** A room with decent-sized tables set up in cluster/cafe style.
- **So What?** Have a plan for how this session is going to impact the world outside the room.

The key element to focus on at this point is that first one: the objective. The objective is where most meetings and workshops fail. People either don't have a clear objective or don't follow it through properly. Remember that LSP is just the method we're using; it serves the objective you and the group are there to achieve.

Here are some common high-level objectives for LSP:

- To open up discussion and explore a topic
- To create a shared understanding of something (e.g., a vision, an issue)

- To develop a broader view of a topic or system
- To decide, as a group, on a course of action to take

To get even more specific, here are some objectives from my LSP sessions:

- To develop a shared understanding of how each team can execute the strategy better. Come out of the session with five actions per team.
- To generate ideas on how we can deliver more value to our internal and external clients.
- To explore areas of innovation that will open up new business opportunities for our division.
- To gain a shared understanding of everyone's role and where they fit into the team.
- To explore and then agree on the team's culture principles.
- To develop a team vision and the concrete steps to get us there.

Throughout this book you'll see the LSP activities and steps that will allow you and your group to dive deeper into a topic. LSP facilitates that deeper conversation and helps you generate new insights and turn them into actions.

4.4 SET UP THE ROOM

You've decided to use LSP. You've got your objective and designed the session.[1] Now it's time to set up the room.

Here's what I do for room setup:

- Room booked thirty minutes beforehand (setup) and thirty minutes afterward (pack-up)
- Table(s) set up in cluster/cafe style. Space for six people per table (if you have more than six people, do multiple tables).
- LEGO pile in the centre of the table
- Tools to capture insights (Post-it notes, flip chart, markers, etc.)
- Slides up on projector or whiteboard/flip charts prepared
- Music ready

HOW MANY TABLES/GROUPS SHOULD I HAVE?

Tables of five to six people work best. The absolute maximum I would have on a table is eight people. Beyond that, the process starts to break down. Here is the way I break up bigger groups:

1 Of course, you've done this after learning the method in chapters 5 through 11 and learning how to design a session in chapter 12.

The ideal setup. Pile of LEGO in the middle, space to build models.

Number of People	Number of Tables
1–8	1
9–14	2
15–19	3
20–24	4
25–30	5

HOW SHOULD I SET UP THE LEGO?

I have a big pile of LEGO in a bag in the centre of the table. This option is good because:

- The LEGO is easily accessible.
- It promotes discovery and exploration of the LEGO pile. This can lead to novel insights when

someone comes across a random piece of LEGO and uses it to mean something.

- It allows ease of setup, moving of LEGO in workshop, pack-up and transport.

> We try to control as many external factors as possible. From the workshop room size and how exposed it is, to the time of the day and whether participants will be hungry or tired, to how formal or informal the setup will be. It all influences the workshop.
>
> —Anders and Bjorn

WHAT LEGO SHOULD I USE?

While you're reading this book and doing the activities yourself, you can use any LEGO you have.

If you are super keen, get a LEGO Serious Play starter kit (2000414) to use. It's available from the LEGO online shop (best price), Amazon or BrickLink.

When you want to use LSP with a group, get six of those LSP starter kits, dump them in a pile and there you have it: a table kit for six people to use.

If you want to get even fancier, read appendix 1: What LEGO to Use, where I discuss the different sets and the different options available to you.

Now that everything is set up, we're ready for our LEGO Serious Play session.

Chapter 5

SESSION INTRODUCTION

> Trust in the process; it won't let you down.
>
> —Aaron

People come to every meeting or workshop with things on their mind—in this case, questions and self-talk such as:

- What is this LEGO Serious Play thing?
- Is it for real or is it just a fun activity?
- How can a kid's toy help me in my work?
- I'm worried that I will fail at this.
- Will I look stupid in front of my colleagues because I'm crap at LEGO?

- I'm not creative.
- I don't like LEGO.

Your role as facilitator is to clear people's minds and allow them to fully engage with the method and the topic. The introduction outlined below does that. The sections in italics are exactly what I say as a facilitator to groups that I'm taking through LSP.

You only need to do this introduction for a group new to LSP. If they know LSP already, you can skip this introduction and go straight to the Skills Building activities in chapter 6.

This introduction may sound very prescriptive, but over the years I've found that if I do it this way, it works every time. Take the words below as a guide and find your voice and your style. As long as you cover the main elements, the group will be ready for the session.

Here are the key elements to address in the first five minutes:

- What is LSP?
- Who uses LSP and why?
- Six bricks activity
- Why LSP is different from LEGO
- Objective of the session

5.1 WHAT IS LSP?

Cover what LSP is and where it came from. Say to the group:

LEGO Serious Play is a method that will help us to think differently and have different conversations.

It was developed by the LEGO Group back in the early 2000s as a way to do strategy by taking it out of the boring world of PowerPoint, reports and spreadsheets and bringing it to life in 3-D.

It's now moved beyond strategy and beyond the LEGO Group.

5.2 WHO USES LSP AND WHY?

We touched on who uses LSP and why they use it in chapter 2.

It's been used by...

I put up a bunch of logos of companies who are using or have used LSP. A few companies from within your industry plus other successful companies is perfect.

The aim here is to show you're not the only ones doing this 'crazy' LEGO thing. It normalises what people are about to do.

I then go on to the why:

> *LEGO Serious Play is used for a range of topics including innovation, customer experience, strategy, change management and much more.*

It's good to include the broad topic that you'll be focusing on too. This shows that what the group are about to do is serious work, not a fun team-building activity.

5.3 SIX BRICKS ACTIVITY

Time to get hands on the bricks.

Most people will not have played with LEGO since childhood. This activity reconnects them with the physical act of putting bricks together and building.

I'll describe what I do in a session, but I want you to follow along and do it too.

> *Dive into the LEGO pile and find six of these "2x4" bricks. Do this individually; each of you grab your own six bricks. Don't worry about the colours.*

Once everyone has their six bricks, tell them to:

The six "2x4" bricks to find. Colour isn't important.

> *Individually, start putting your own six bricks together. Connect them into one model.*
>
> *Once you've done that, dismantle it and put the six bricks together in a different way. Keep doing that for the next thirty seconds.*

After about fifteen seconds, tell them:

> *As you're doing that, think of how many different ways you could combine those six bricks. Any guesses on how many different combinations there are?*

Ask for some guesses.

> *Here is the exact number: 915,103,765 different ways you can combine just those six bricks. With those six bricks, you could build almost a billion different things!*

5.4 WHY LSP IS DIFFERENT FROM LEGO

It's important to shift people's thinking from what they know LEGO is to how they are going to use it in LSP.

> *Now put those bricks back in the pile. Look at that pile. It's not six bricks, it's over a thousand bricks. And not just the standard LEGO bricks, but a whole range of different LEGO pieces. DUPLO, technic and all sorts of different-shaped LEGO.*
>
> *That pile of bricks has an almost infinite number of combinations. You could build and represent anything with that LEGO in front of you.*
>
> *But that's not too surprising. We know that's what the LEGO system is all about. Building whatever you want. Kids have been doing that for over fifty years. So how does that help us in business?*
>
> *Let's look at what kids build with LEGO. What do they build?*

Ask the group. You'll usually get back answers like cars, spaceships, castles and houses.

What is the common thing about all those items?

Ask for answers.

The common thing is that they are all literal, real objects that you can see and touch out there. That is the outside world.

But here is where LEGO Serious Play is different. We're not going to build the outside world; we're going to build the inside world. The world inside your mind.

I point at my head to reinforce the point. Usually people look at me a little strangely.

There are ideas, opinions, experiences all floating around in your mind. We're going to give them form in a LEGO model. Put them on the table and have a conversation about them. That's LEGO Serious Play.

It's like 3-D printing your mind, your ideas. Taking ideas from your head and putting them on the table. Using them to have a better conversation.

So LEGO is just the tool, the medium we will use. But LEGO Serious Play is the steps and processes that help us get those ideas out of our head and onto the table.

5.5 OBJECTIVE OF THE SESSION

At this point I like to remind people that LEGO Serious Play is simply the method we will use.

But remember, LEGO Serious Play is the method. What we're here to focus on today is [insert your objective here]. And the bricks will help us to do that.

> When setting up the workshop, ensure that everyone understands that LEGO Serious Play is a method that is going to be used to achieve a workshop goal. It is not the focus of the workshop itself.
>
> —Jacky

Everything I explained earlier encompasses the five-minute introduction that gets people ready for Skills Building. Remember the key items to address are:

- What is LSP?
- Who uses LSP and why?
- Six bricks activity
- Why LSP is different from LEGO
- Objective of the session

Chapter 6

SKILLS BUILDING

After the introduction, your participants should have many of their questions answered. They're now ready to dive into LSP.

The first thing you, as facilitator, need to do is get the group to learn and practise this new method. We call this section Skills Building because we're building up the group's skills in LSP. Once they are warmed up to the method, then you can dive into the topic of the session.

For a group new to LSP, the set of Skills Building activities takes around twenty-five minutes. For a group that already know LSP, you still need to do a Skills Building activity to get them back into 'LSP mode', but it can be a lot shorter (I've detailed some options at the end of this chapter).

6.1 WHY DO YOU NEED TO DO SKILLS BUILDING?

Spending twenty-five minutes getting people up to speed is a time investment. But if you skip Skills Building or try to do it more quickly, the rest of the process falls down. That up-front investment pays off with better insights and better outcomes.

Remember that the aim of Skills Building is to get everyone to understand the process of LEGO Serious Play and ready to engage with the real questions using this new skill.

In seven years of doing this Skills Building process, it has never failed me. Here's what I do in every session for a new group.

6.2 THE FOUR STEPS OF LEGO SERIOUS PLAY

Straight after the introduction, I outline these four steps. Here is what I say to the group:

There are four steps to the LEGO Serious Play method:

1. *Question*
2. *Build*
3. *Share*
4. *Capture*

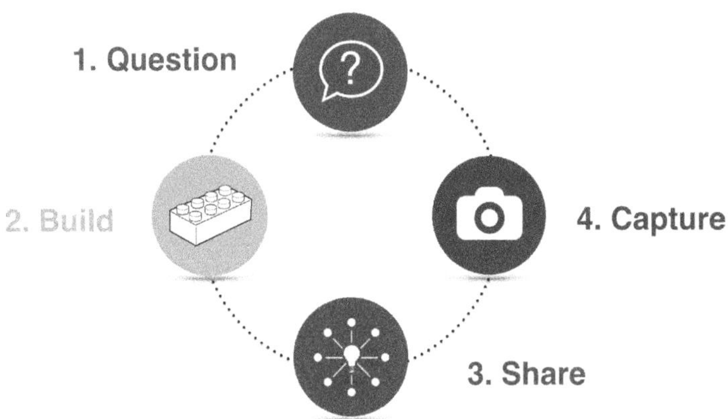

The four steps of LEGO Serious Play[2]

STEP 1: QUESTION

For Step 1, I will ask you a question. It will be on the topic we're here to talk about today.

A question like: [for example] What is your vision for this team over the next two years?

STEP 2—BUILD

In Step 2, you build your answer to that question in LEGO.

2 Yes, this circle is going counter-clockwise. When I first designed this image in 2014, I didn't consciously make it that way. But subconsciously, I was clearly channelling the counter-cultureness of the method. When it was pointed out to me a few years later, I thought it seemed fitting to leave it going in the opposite direction to expectations.

You build it individually. This is not some team-building activity where you build a bridge and get over it together. This is your individual answer in model form.

I'll play some music. You'll have five minutes to build a model that is your answer to the question.

Some people freak out at this point, thinking 'I'm not good at building with LEGO' or 'I'm not that creative'. The great thing is that it doesn't matter! There's no right or wrong, good or bad.

It doesn't matter how you build in Step 2. The next step, Step 3, is the important one.

STEP 3: SHARE

In Step 3, you share the story of your model.

I usually pick someone out.

So Matt spends one or two minutes sharing the story of his model, which is his answer to the question.

Everyone else at his table listens. When Matt finishes, you can ask questions to help get more insights. Perhaps Matt forgets to explain a small part of his model. You could ask a clarifying question, like, 'Does that red brick have any meaning'?

Maybe you want to know more about a particular part: 'Tell me more about this part of the model…'.

Your aim as a group is to be curious and help Matt tell a great story full of insights. Then move on to the next person at the table and do the same thing. Share the story and ask questions, all the way around the table.

After everyone has told their story, it's important to end this step with a reflection of what happened. As a group, reflect on what you all saw and heard and what you all learned.

STEP 4: CAPTURE

Step 4 is capturing all those insights from your discussion.

I like to do this by getting each of you to write down an insight on one of these cards and then take a photo of your model.

We will go through that cycle a few times over the session: Question, Build, Share, Capture, but with different questions that take us deeper into the topic.

A little later on, we will do more group activities where we build some of these models together into a group model. But for now, we'll start with individual work.

6.3 TIPS

Alongside these four steps, there are a couple of tips that I've found helpful.

Tip 1

I'm going to assume that everyone here in the room is a smart person. What happens when you ask a smart person a complex question? What do you do first when you're in a meeting and someone asks a complex question?

The first thing you do is think. That's what you're paid to do. That's why you have a job: your ability to analyse, to think. But when faced with a pile of LEGO, that's the wrong thing to do.

Here is the first tip: don't have a meeting with yourself!

Don't overthink it. If I ask you a question and you don't know the answer, I don't want to see you staring out the window contemplating the answer or grabbing a pen and sketching out what you're going to build.

If you don't know what to build, put your hands in the LEGO and start building.

There's great science that shows that our hands are connected to our brains in more ways than we realise. More than any other part of our body. People who use their hands are better problem solvers. So let your hands help you to find the answer.

Don't have a meeting with yourself!

Tip 2

The second tip I have for you is: think in metaphor and story.

What does that mean?

You could build cars, houses, castles, trains and spaceships. That's fine. But when you build with metaphor and story, amazing insights come out.

Here are three examples:

This black brick is my favourite brick. It has studs on the side as well as the top. It is a very functional brick. But the reason I like it is the metaphor and story behind it.

I was doing an LSP workshop for the Asylum Seeker Resource Centre in my home city. The participants had built all these wonderful models of different stakeholders.

My favourite brick. It was used in a session to represent fear.

The asylum seeker, the resource centre, the government, the person who donates. All there in LEGO.

Then one gentleman grabbed this brick (the black brick) and said this brick is fear. And proceeded to connect it to each model and show how the asylum seeker is fearful. How the resource centre is fearful. How the government is fearful.

For him (and us) that brick became fear.

The key insight here is that the bricks can be whatever you want them to be.

Take a simple bit of spiky LEGO grass. It could be just grass or an obvious metaphor, like environment or sustainability. But what if we put it on top of a Minifigure's head?

Suddenly it becomes an explosion of ideas, innovation, creativity. Instead of it being on top, maybe the Minifigure is sitting on the grass. Except it's not grass; it's a spiky situation and this is a metaphor for a problem this person is facing.

Another example is this tower I built with me in it. Let me share the story and the metaphors.

At the bottom, you can see some different-coloured bricks or steps.

OPPOSITE: My tower with me in it. My work, my family, my purpose.

The red brick represents my passion, enthusiasm and energy for what I do. The green one is my curiosity and growth. The blue one is my analytical/tech side. The clear one is my motto for this year: radical transparency.

All those steps lead up to that round black platform. That is the LEGO Serious Play method. It's supporting me and my family: my partner (on the right), my daughter (in the middle) and me, with two heads.

One of those heads has a flower on it. That represents new ideas. I see my strength and my role as sparking new ideas in both myself and the people in my workshops. The other head has a crash helmet on it. I play a protective role for both my family and the LSP method.

The white column with grass on top is my ultimate goal. That is flourishing for me as a human, for my family and for the people in my workshops.

That's my tower and all the metaphor and story within it. Remember the bricks can be whatever you want them to be.

> Make sure that all the attendees understand the basics of building and describing things in stories and metaphors.
>
> —Jacky

I've learnt over the years that this part of LSP is key. The group need to 'get' the whole build-in-metaphor thing. That's why I put in three examples (fear brick, grass and my tower).

Remember that in chapter 2, I mentioned that if people end up building in a very literal way for your LSP session, then the method loses a lot of its power. This part of Skills Building is key.

You'll know if you've got it right when the group do the first activity below, building a tower. If you see a lot of very literal, simple towers, then the group haven't quite got the whole metaphor thing. Some literal towers are okay; a few people take time to warm up to this idea. But if the majority of people are building literal towers, then the group haven't got it yet.

If you follow the above and give examples, then you will very rarely have any problems.

I use those three examples above (fear brick, grass and my tower) all the time. You're quite welcome to use them. But also feel free to use your own examples. You'll start to gather your own fascinating stories from LSP sessions. Use those, use your tower, use your favourite bricks and examples.

6.4 ACTIVITY: 'BUILD A TOWER WITH YOU IN IT'

Now we're going to do a Skills Building activity. I want you to build a tower with you in it.

I don't want to see anyone getting up on the table and trying to climb into their tower. But something representing you has to be in the tower. It can be from work, home, hobby, whatever you like.

You've got three minutes, and remember to not have a meeting with yourself.

The activity again is to build a tower with you in it.

I put on some music. The song that I play for this activity is 'Sweet Disposition' by a band called Temper Trap. I'll discuss my music choices in more depth in the next chapter.

You're halfway done. One and a half minutes to go...

Thirty seconds to go...

And that is time.

A quick reminder: we did Step 1, where I asked you to build a tower with you in it. You built it in Step 2 and now we're up to Step 3, which is Share.

On each table, someone brave can start. Take one to two minutes to tell the story of your model. Everyone else will listen and then ask some questions to help get more insights. Then the next person tells their story.

I encourage you, the reader, to share your model and story with someone else. There's also a place at *www.lspmethod.com/book* to post a photo and write your story.

Once everyone has told their story, ask:

What did you see and hear? What insights did you have? Reflect on this and discuss as a group.

Give the group a minute or two to reflect and discuss.

Now it's time to capture those wonderful insights and models. Write down on a card one insight you had from the discussion. It can be a single word, a hashtag, a sentence or a whole essay.

After you've written that, take a photo of your tower. Then dismantle your tower and put the LEGO back in the pile.

Now you know how to do LEGO Serious Play. Let's move on to the topic for today...

At this point you, as facilitator, transition the group to the first individual build, which you'll learn about in the next chapter.

That is how you run the Skills Building section!

6.5 RECAP

- **Introduce the Four Steps.** Question, Build, Share, Capture.
- **Highlight the Two tips.** 'Don't have a meeting with yourself' and 'think in metaphor and story'. Make sure to include examples.
- **Build a Tower with You in It** activity

6.6 THE POWER OF BUILDING A TOWER

This 'build a tower with you in it' activity is a powerful opening to an LSP session.

Over hundreds of sessions, I have had a few people cry as they are telling the story of their tower, because it's a very personal question. You are building yourself and putting a part of yourself out there. For these people, the activity is often very cathartic. They are being heard.

Their issue or their current state is right there in physical form in front of them. They always move through it and continue with the session. It's never a bad thing, but you do need to be aware it can happen and act with empathy.

This highlights the fact that this activity is no mere warm-up. It's a deeply personal question that opens many people up. The good thing is that the activity allows people to adjust their level of openness. Some build a tower and reveal a minor thing about themselves. That's fine. They've still achieved what we wanted them to. Others can go deep. That's fine too. Don't be surprised if you hear some deeply personal things in this activity.

6.7 SECOND-TIME GROUPS

If a group already know LSP and have done the tower, you still need to warm them up. Here are two other options:

OPTION 1: EXPLAIN THIS!

My favourite way to warm people up again is with an activity called 'Explain This!' This is a quick little activity that gets people back into building and metaphor mode.

Before the session, write some interesting topics on a set of cards. Do one topic per card and have a card for each participant at a table. You can theme the topics, but I like random topic ideas:

- Democracy
- 1970s
- Social Media
- Artificial Intelligence
- Donald Trump
- The Future of Humanity

Here are the instructions:

1. Get everyone to choose ten LEGO pieces (Minifigures count as one).
2. Get each person to build a model with their ten pieces (two minutes).
3. Hand out a card with a topic on it to each person.
4. Tell them that the topic on the card is what they built (their model is 'social media' or 'democracy').
5. Give them one to two minutes in silence to come up with a story relating their model to that topic.
6. Everyone shares the story of their model.

Remember that this activity is simply to warm participants up. It's a great way to get back into story and metaphor mode. It's fun and people come up with some crazy things, but don't expect long involved stories. Short, sharp and then on to the real questions.

OPTION 2: RANDOM QUESTION

Another option is to get each person to build their answer to a random question, not related to the topic you're going to discuss. In essence, you're getting them to do an Individual Model build, which you will learn more about in the next chapter. It is simply the same four steps you're now familiar with, but instead of a tower, you get to ask an interesting question. Great questions to ask are about their best customer experience; best leader they've worked for; a talent or strength they have outside of work; or what they're excited about at the moment.

It's important that this warm-up question is not related to the main topic. The purpose of this build is to warm people up, and you don't want to dive too quickly into the main topic.

6.8 GALLERY

Over the next few chapters, I'll be sharing with you some models from sessions. I'm always wary about recording people's stories from sessions, for fear of breaking the magic of LEGO Serious Play. Below you'll get my version of the highlights from each model. But know that the stories behind all of these models are richer, more powerful and, when heard firsthand, much more captivating.

TOWER 1

This person's tower has multiple legs. Each one is a different income stream that supports her. The legs allow her to branch off in many different directions to pursue what she loves (those colourful pieces sticking out halfway up).

Because of those different legs, she's never stuck or beholden to one thing. They allow her to support the important things in her life: family, flexibility and security (the flower and the two pink posts).

TOWER 2

The model builder explained, 'I like my tower to be open. Open sides, open window, binoculars to see far.'

That string connector on the left is so this person can stay connected to the outside world, and it allows a path for people to come in. The net that is part of the roof is again about openness: wanting some filter between herself and the outside world, but a filter that lets a lot though.

An interesting feature of this tower is that it doesn't look much like a tower! That's fine; you will see towers of all shapes and sizes. The point of using 'tower' as the prompt is that it's a flexible enough concept that people can mould it to what they want it to be.

OPPOSITE: Tower 1: An abstract tower.

Family
Security

TOP: Tower 2: An open, flat tower. BOTTOM: Tower 3: A prison tower. OPPOSITE: Tower 4: A clear tower with no people

TOWER 3

The model builder reflected on what they had built: 'I don't like what that's saying.'

Sometimes people's towers look like prisons. It happens occasionally in my corporate workshops. It's okay. People achieve the aim of the activity and express that they're a little stuck.

The builder of this one represented themselves as a skeleton, looking out at the nice flower outside (representing what they would rather be doing). Their career goal was there (the cup on top) but blocked off from them. They can see out, but cannot get out.

TOWER 4

This tower is a bit more open. The pink flower represents opportunity and, while there is a door, it can only be opened with some work. The yellow bricks with eyes are scanning the outside environment and the cog underneath the flower is this person's skills and ability to achieve. All of this is built on a base of transparent blue bricks, which represent a calm approach.

6.9 LAST THOUGHTS ON SKILLS BUILDING

Skills building is a vital part of an LSP session. Follow the steps, spend the time to get it right and it will pay dividends during the session.

Chapter 7

INDIVIDUAL MODELS

Now that the group are warmed up through the Skills Building activity, it's time to get to the real questions!

LEGO Serious Play is a toolkit of activities that you mix and match to form a session.

There are three main activities.

- **Individual Models**. People build their own model in response to a question.
- **Shared Models.** The group combines the Individual Models to form a group model.
- **Landscape Models**. The group keep the Individual Models intact and arrange them on the table to show relationships using space and placement.

These three activities are flexible enough to tackle almost any topic. There is a chapter on how to facilitate each one. There are a couple of other activities within the LEGO Serious Play toolkit, and these are covered in chapter 10.

All LSP sessions are simply some combination of these activities. For now, it's important to learn how to run the activities, and then, in chapter 12, we'll put them together to form a session.

7.1 INDIVIDUAL MODEL OVERVIEW

The Individual Model activity is the core activity of the LSP method; all the other activities are built upon it. It's always the first thing you do after the Skills Building. It's important to ask for people's individual answers first, giving them a chance to share their thoughts before moving into group work.

The great thing is that you already know this activity. You experienced it when you built the tower in the previous chapter. The Individual Model activity follows the same four steps: Question, Build, Share, Capture. In the Individual Model context, the difference is that the question asked and what people build is focused on the objective for the session.

7.2 PRACTISE

The best way to understand and get better at LSP is to experience it. Grab some LEGO and let's do an Individual Model activity. Choose a number between one and six.

Got your number?

Here is your question for Individual Model building:

1. What is your vision for your career over the next five years?
2. What superpower do you bring to work?
3. What value do you bring to your clients?
4. Think of a time you had an amazing customer experience. What made it amazing (the key factors) and why?
5. Think of a time you've been part of a successful team or project. What factors drove that success?
6. What's a current challenge you are facing in your career?

Put some music on. Spend five minutes building your model. Share the story of your model with someone else. You can share it online, too, at *www.lspmethod.com/book*.

7.3 INDIVIDUAL MODEL STEPS

Shortly, I'll go over how to facilitate this activity. But first, a note on questions: the questions above are a small sample of what you could ask. You already have dozens and dozens of questions you're asking yourself in your work. That's what work is: answering questions and using that information to take action. Many of those questions could be used in an LSP session.

In chapter 12, I'll cover what makes a great LSP question and how to find the best ones. For now, know there are many potential questions you could ask using this activity.

Here is your role in each of the four steps of the Individual Model activity:

STEP 1: QUESTION

You decide on and design all the questions of a session beforehand. This step is about delivering that question in a very clear way. You want to do that by both verbalising the question to participants *and* having it written out somewhere visible to them. Many times I've had people look up halfway through building to check the wording of the question again.

Tell people how long they have. I like five minutes for building, but you can do shorter or longer (there is a more in-depth discussion on 'build time' later in this chapter). Ask for any questions. Then, the last thing participants should hear before they start building is the question again. You are repeating the question again in the space of twenty seconds, but that is okay. It's better for everyone to be clear.

STEP 2: BUILD

Encourage people to get building, and keep an eye out for anyone who is struggling.

I like to play music during the Build step. My music of choice is best described as an 'inspirational running mix' (it used to be the list I ran to). It's upbeat but melts into the background. You want it to enable, not distract. The volume should allow people to have a conversation, although they shouldn't during this step!

I've got my list below, but play whatever feels right for you. I've tried other styles of music, like classical, particular decades (e.g., eighties, nineties), new releases. What I've found is that a lot of music distracts, polarises, sends people to sleep, gets them out of flow and so on. You want something that either is neutral or inspires the whole group, not just some of the group. Start with this list and evolve it from there:

- 'Sweet Disposition' by Temper Trap
- 'Blame It on Me' by George Ezra

- 'Bohemian Like You' by The Dandy Warhols
- 'Riptide' by Vance Joy
- 'Young Blood' by The Naked and Famous
- 'Happy' by Pharrell Williams
- 'Don't Hold Back' by The Potbelleez
- 'Headlights' by Robin Schulz
- 'Call It What You Want' by Foster the People
- 'Levels' by Avicii
- 'I Need a Dollar' by Aloe Blacc

In the first minute of the build, scan the group to see if anyone is stuck. This usually happens when people are overthinking the question. I put in a gentle reminder to the whole group: 'Don't have a meeting with yourself. Put your hands on the LEGO and let it help you to answer the question'.

Also, keep an eye out for anyone struggling with the technical aspect of LEGO. Occasionally, people can't get certain bricks to connect, and you don't want them to get stuck on that. Reassure them: 'I'm here to help if anyone needs technical advice'.

The other key role you play is timekeeper. My standard time for an Individual Model build is five minutes. I do verbal time checks. Don't put a countdown clock on the screen. It's stressful and changes the way people build.

Halfway through, I say, 'That's halfway. You have two and a half minutes left'. I announce again when they have one minute to go and finally at thirty seconds.

The little trick here is those timings aren't fixed. In other words, I adjust them in the moment depending on how the group is going. If I notice the group struggling to finish, quite often that last minute ends up being two minutes. It's a balance, though, because you could let people go on and build ridiculously complex, intricate models. But we're trying to promote spontaneous thinking where the model is just a prompt (even if unfinished).

STEP 3: SHARE

> Give more time for sharing. Never underestimate the benefit of taking time to explain models and then push deeper with good reflective questions.
>
> —Ben

Your role changes depending on whether you have one table or multiple tables. Here, I'll focus on one table and what your role is. Later in this chapter, I'll show you what to do with multiple tables.

Your role is to facilitate participants sharing stories:

1. State the question again. For example, 'What you built was your vision for the team. Let's now move to the Share step. Spend a minute or two telling us about your model. Nicole, do you want to go first?'
2. After the first person has told the story of their model, open it up to the group: 'Are there any questions, comments or reflections about Nicole's model and story?' It's important to let the group ask their questions first. You want them to drive the discussion. If no one has any questions, you can jump in with yours.
3. I like to ask two different types of questions: clarifying and probing.
   a. Clarifying. 'Does that orange brick on top have any meaning?' Sometimes a brick is just a brick and has no meaning. But sometimes it does. So always ask.
   b. Probing. 'Tell me more about that part of the model.' Or 'You mentioned collaboration, tell me more about that'.
4. Avoid asking 'why' questions (e.g., 'Why did you build that part?'). Why questions ask for reasons

and they often put people on the defensive as they search for justification for their actions. LSP works because you are creating psychological safety in the group. Asking why questions can break that safety and lead to people closing off.

5. Don't let the share go on too long. You only have time to ask around three to four questions per model.
6. If you like, you, as facilitator, can do a one-sentence summary of the person's story (e.g., 'So your model and story was about...'), but this part is optional. It can be helpful if the story was long and detailed.
7. I like to thank the person for their story and model.
8. Repeat the above steps for each person.

Once everyone has shared their story, I finish this step off with a group reflection.

I ask:

- 'What did you all see and hear?'
- 'Were there any themes that came out?'
- 'What were the key insights for you?'

> Remember you are a facilitator. Do not provide personal opinions or direct their answers in any way. Go with the participants' flow, help them elaborate on the models and always be flexible. Sometimes, the best insights come from moments you have not planned.
>
> —Gabu

STEP 4: CAPTURE

Ensure people capture the insights in the way you want. My preferred way is for people to write their insights on cards and take photos of their models. You can use small cards like the ones you see in some of my photos or large index cards. The bigger the card, the more people will write. Play around with card size to find what level of 'capture' works for you. For a long time, I used small cards, but in recent workshops I've started using bigger cards, and I'm enjoying the added detail that people are including.

Other options to capture insights include a flip chart or whiteboard, videos and audio recordings.

I've found that people are great at taking photos, but the photos are then stuck in their phones. To gather all these photos together as a group, I use an online service called *Padlet*, which allows people to post their photos into a secure online gallery. After everyone has shared their stories, written down an insight on a card and taken a photo, I get each person to go to the Padlet website and upload their photo. Posting these photos as you go means that by the end of the session you have a wonderful group record of what happened in the session.

As people are capturing their insights on cards and with photos, mention to the group whether you want them to keep or dismantle their models. Usually, you want them to keep the models to do further activities with, such as Shared Models and Landscape Models.

7.4 BUILD TIME

One of the bigger decisions you need to make as a facilitator is how long you will let people build. My preferred time is five minutes for an Individual Model. This strikes a nice balance between allowing enough time to get the model done and encouraging an instinctive style of thinking and building. It suits the type of sessions I run, and I find that it leads to interesting, novel insights.

Of course, you can vary that build time. If the question is really complex or you want more deliberate thinking in the group, you can allow longer. I sometimes go up to eight or nine minutes.

You can also go the other way and allow less time. One of my favourite things to do is give people only two minutes to build and then get them to put that model to the side and do another two-minute build. I usually do this when I want to get multiple answers from each participant. It works perfectly for a question like, 'What are the challenges you are facing in this project'? Build one quickly, then another (and another if you want). It's a fun form of ideation to get lots of answers out.

If in doubt, go with five-minute builds. But know that as you get comfortable with the LSP method, you can vary this time to get different results.

7.5 BIGGER GROUPS

As mentioned in the pre-session details back in chapter 4, tables of five to six people are best. If you have more than eight people in the group, you will need to run multiple tables. Your role as facilitator changes when you do that.

When there is one table, I like to sit at the table with the group and facilitate from there. When there are multiple tables, the facilitator can't be present at all of them, all of the time; the tables need to be a little more self-directed. Here is what I do:

- **Step 1 (Question)**. Same as for a single table. But deliver the same question and instructions to the whole group.[3]
- **Step 2 (Build)**. Same as for a single table. But keep an eye across all the tables for anyone struggling.
- **Step 3 (Share)**. Give the usual instructions that each person will have two to three minutes to tell their story. Encourage others to ask questions and then let each table run this step themselves. Keep an eye out across the tables to see if anything is going wrong, and pop in to listen for a short time at each table. You'll also need to ensure that each table is moving through the process at a steady pace. Sometimes a story hog will take a long time to tell their story and will slow one table down. If you notice this happening, a gentle instruction to the whole group to 'Make sure to keep moving it along so that everyone can share their story' usually helps to speed up the slower tables.
- **Step 4 (Capture)**. Same as for a single table.

3 There is a more advanced approach in which you can ask each table a different question. The advantage is that the group get through more work, but it can be complicated to integrate. For now, just picture each table doing the same question.

7.6 GALLERY

To give you a better idea of what people build using the Individual Model activity, I've included four Individual Model builds from different sessions. Again, I'll be giving you my recollections of participants' stories, which are nowhere near the depth of the original stories. But it does give you a feel for what to expect from this activity.

INDIVIDUAL MODEL 1

'What strengths do you bring to the team?'

The model builder is the Minifigure at the base of that white column. They see their strengths as connecting people and innovation. They are lifting up their colleagues (the other Minifigures) and connecting them via ideas (that's why the others have things attached to their heads).

Through sparking new ideas, this person is lifting their colleagues up out of their mundane work tasks (the items on the ground: pink bricks, net, etc.) so they can think clearly and see a long way.

The end result is that giving people the space to think new ideas and the time to connect on those ideas will help the team to flourish (the grass on top).

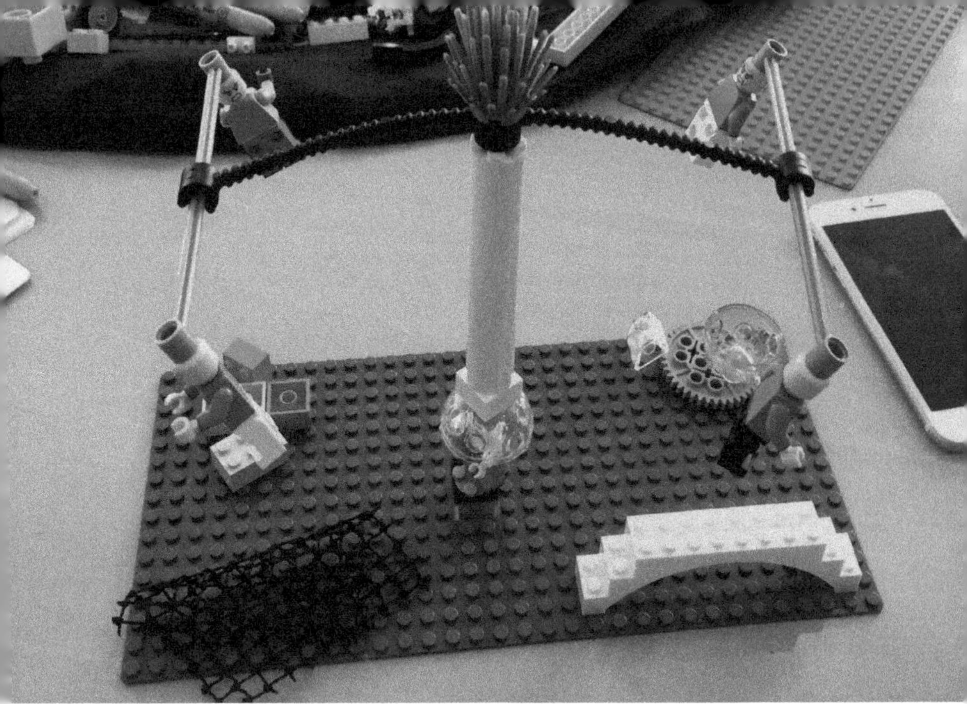

Individual Model 1: An Individual Model from a team identity workshop.

INDIVIDUAL MODEL 2

'What is your vision for the _____ team?'

This was a model of transformation from bottom to top. The cow represented past successes. The team have been very successful and are sometimes seen as a cash cow. The cow leads up to the wheel, which represents change (the model did actually spin around on that wheel, although precariously, which fit in nicely with the vision).

Above that is the need to create a platform, inverted from the normal. On top of that is the tiger, showing competitiveness and the need to look to the outside for opportunities. The three globes represent DNA and the

idea that competitiveness and vision need to become part of who they are.

INDIVIDUAL MODEL 3

'What is the internal identity of the company?'

This person worked in a small remote office of fifteen people as part of a large multinational company. Their model represents both the gap and the connections back to head office.

The head office is represented by the big window with the dog in it. The dog represents play, which this company is known for. The person at the front has 'eyes in all directions of trends', which was the role of this remote office.

The blue represented the water (and gap) between the two, and a ladder represented a bridge connecting the two. While there were communication challenges in this setup, overall it worked well.

INDIVIDUAL MODEL 4

'What are the challenges facing LinkedIn?'

This was from a case study done with students at an education company called General Assembly. The students

OPPOSITE: Individual Model 2: An Individual Model from a team vision workshop.

TOP: Individual Model 3: An Individual Model from a company strategy session. BELOW: Individual Model 4: An Individual Model from a case study class.

were doing a case study of different businesses, their challenges and their opportunities.

The model builder explained:

These are all the profiles that people have on LinkedIn. Some are dressed up; some are sort of fake (the skeleton). There's lots of distraction on LinkedIn (the red tube on the right), which takes you away from the reason for being there.

This is a premium user (the Minifigure on the platform on the left) and the prize, which is a job, is on the other platform on the right. The premium user has a better view of the prize, but still no direct path.

7.7 LAST THOUGHTS ON INDIVIDUAL MODELS

Individual Models are the core of the LEGO Serious Play method. They are how you engage everyone and tap into rich, deep experiences and stories.

The rest of the LSP method builds on these Individual Models, finding the connections, the relationships, moving these ideas around and changing participants' thinking. But all of that relies on good Individual Models. As a person who is learning LSP for the first time, you should focus on doing this activity well, and the rest of the activities will have a solid foundation.

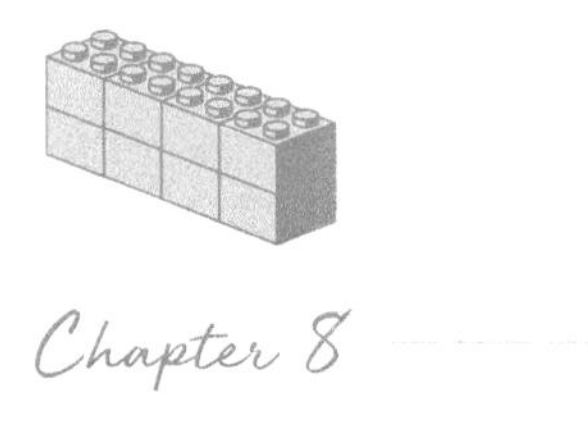

Chapter 8

SHARED MODELS

You could run an entire LEGO Serious Play session using the Individual Model activity you just learnt. But with that activity, you only get individual answers. Sometimes you want to dive deeper, see connections and get a group answer.

That's where Shared Models and Landscape Models come in. They take Individual Models and combine and rearrange them to get fresh perspectives and insights.

The Shared Model activity does this by pulling models apart and recombining them.

The Landscape Model activity does this by keeping the models intact but arranging them on the table to show relationships (see chapter 9).

8.1 SHARED MODEL OVERVIEW

A Shared Model is created when a group takes their Individual Models and puts them together to create one group model with one story.

This process involves:

- Discussing what should be included from the Individual Models and what should be left out
- Pulling parts off Individual Models and combining elements from different Individual Models
- Testing out different configurations to see what the group can agree on

Through this process, the group challenge their individual ideas and integrate them to see if they are fit for the final group model. The end result is a model and story full of novel insights and connections that the group are far more invested in. They built it, they own it.

As this activity unfolds, you'll often hear people saying things like:

- 'I like that bit of your model; let's take that off yours and include it in the group model.'
- 'Three of us included a theme around collaboration in our Individual Models; how do

> we want to represent that in the group model? I like the way you represented it, so let's include that but with this small element from mine that helps to round it out.'

The key feature of a Shared Model is that you can pull parts off your Individual Model, but the meaning of those bricks must stay the same. If your LEGO grass meant creativity, it has to mean creativity in the final group model. But you can pull it off your Individual Model and put it in a new place in the group model.

This Shared Model activity is commonly used in strategy or vision development. People build Individual Models of the vision they see for the company or team. Then, through the Shared Model activity, the group come up with one vision model that everyone agrees on.

You can use the Shared Model activity to address many other topics for which it makes sense to combine Individual Models and get a group answer. Other examples of good topics for Shared Models include:

- **Team Culture**. 'What do you want team life to be like in the future?'
- **Innovation**. 'What does the innovation journey look like here at XXXX?'

- **Value Proposition**. 'What's our value proposition?'
- **Leadership**. 'What are the key ingredients of good leadership?'

8.2 SHARED MODEL STEPS

To facilitate a Shared Model activity, begin by building Individual Models.

The group go through the standard Individual Model activity (Question, Build, Share, Capture). They are then ready to run a Shared Model activity using the models they've built.

The high-level steps of a Shared Model match the Question, Build, Share, Capture process you're familiar with. But the details in each step and your role as facilitator changes quite a bit.

STEP 1: QUESTION

The group have finished their Individual Models. They've shared their stories. They've captured their insights. Their models are on the table in front of them.

As facilitator, you guide them by saying:

You have all built models of [insert your topic here]. Now it's time to bring them together.

Show the group the question. It's virtually the same question they just built, but this time we want a group answer.

> *The question is: Combine your models into one group model showing your vision for the team. It's not about including everything. It's about having a discussion and deciding what's important and what's not: what gets included and what gets left out. You can pull models apart and combine them with others. Some of your own model will make it in; some of it won't. That's okay. It's about coming up with the best group answer.*
>
> *The only rule is that the meaning of the bricks must stay the same. For example, if I used a DUPLO lion to mean 'we all need to have courage', when we go to build, we can't repurpose the lion to mean something else (like a threat). The meaning of your models stays the same. But you can and should pull parts off your model to include in the group model.*

I've found the best way to start this activity is with a recap of each person's story.

> *To kick things off, go around the table again and, in one or two sentences, recap your Individual Model for everyone as a reminder.*

Once they've done the recap, give the group a couple of "32x32 baseplates" (large LEGO boards) on which they will build their Shared Model.

There's no time limit for this activity. It normally takes around thirty to forty minutes, depending on the topic and numbers in the group.

STEP 2: BUILD

After the recap of stories, let the group know it's time to build. You, as facilitator, should take a step back.

The first few minutes can be a little awkward for the group. They are figuring out how to come together and do this new activity. You will be tempted to jump in and help. Don't do it too early. Let that uncomfortableness sit with them. It will surprise you how the group come together to start forming their model.

If you do want to give them a helping hand at the start, I've found this little prompt very useful: 'What do you like about someone else's Individual Model? What of theirs would you like to see included?' This usually gets things moving.

This is a great example of your role in this step. Stand back and only jump in when the process is going off track. I call these interventions 'nudges': subtle little questions or prompts that help get the process back on track.

As facilitator, you're not there to add your view. Focus on nudges, prompts and questions to help the process. It's not your role to give opinions, judgements or recommendations on the content of the discussion. The moment you add your view, the story isn't the group's anymore and the magic is broken.

Some common nudges or prompts that I use are:

- 'Let's hear from others in the group.'—To get a different perspective and change the flow of conversation.
- 'How do we show that in the model?'—When the group slip back into talking meeting mode instead of building.
- 'What are you as a group struggling with?'—If the group get stuck.

For the first part of the Shared Model activity, you are standing back and nudging when necessary.

About three-quarters of the way through, your role changes. The Shared Model is forming, but the group haven't quite finished it yet. Your new role is to help the group refine their model. I do this through a series of questions and instructions.

Devil's Advocate

One of the potential pitfalls of this activity is groupthink or including everything from every model. This is where the Devil's Advocate activity helps.

> *For the next five minutes, I want each of you to play devil's advocate. What don't you like about this model? What should we remove? What are we not talking about? You don't have to change your model. But have the discussion and then decide if you need to make a change.*

This gives participants permission to voice any doubts they may have.

Persona

Guide the group by saying: 'Imagine you're a customer. How does this Shared Model look to you?' You can insert any other relevant persona (CEO, CFO, internal client, employee, supplier).

Quiet Time

Get everyone to look back at their own models for a minute and see if there's anything still there that they want to include. This gives people a little space to think other thoughts, rather than get lost in the flow of conversation.

Move Around

Get everyone to move and walk around the model, looking from table level to helicopter view at different angles. A new perspective is one advantage of adding a visual component to the conversation.

These activities shake up the building process and allow new insights to surface. You don't need to do them all. My favourite at the moment is Devil's Advocate + Move Around. Find the ones that work best for you.

STEPS 3 AND 4: SHARE AND CAPTURE

When you have one group and they build a Shared Model, you might wonder 'who's left to share it with'? The Share and Capture steps are still important even if you only have one group.

The key is to get the group to tell the story of their Shared Model several times. This is another form of refinement and a way to make sure the story and model make sense to every member of the group.

After the group finish the build, get the group to practise telling the full story of the model. It's a group storytelling effort. One person starts, but everyone needs to jump in at some point to contribute.

Once the group have told the story, get them to do it again. As the group are telling the story for a second (and final) time, capture a video on your phone as a record of the work done in the session.

Once the story has been told and captured, it's important to take a step back as a group and reflect on the activity. I ask these two questions:

- 'What did you see and hear in that activity?'
- 'What were the key insights for you?'

8.3 MULTIPLE TABLES

Your facilitation changes slightly when you have multiple tables.

The Question and Build steps are the same as described in 8.2 above. Groups build their own Shared Model on each table.

When it comes time to share and capture the story, do the same as above, with one little twist. Get people to practise their story at their own table, but then have each table tell their story to another table.

This can take on different formats, depending on the number of tables.

If you have five or fewer tables, get everyone to go over to table 1. Table 1 will share their story. People will ask questions. Then everyone moves on to table 2. Repeat.

If you have six or more tables, pair the tables up. Table 1 shares with table 2. At the same time, table 3 shares with table 4, and table 5 shares with table 6. Then switch. Participants at table 2 tell their story to table 1, those at table 4 tell the story to table 3 and so on.

One question I always get is 'Can you put all those Shared Models together into one mega Shared Model?' My experience is no, not reliably.

The challenge is that you have four or five rich Shared Models with their own stories. How do you physically, metaphorically and story-wise combine those with twenty-five or thirty people standing around? The physical logistics are awkward.

What I do instead is a 'global debrief'. I bring all the themes together as a discussion with the whole group. From this, the entire group get a sense of what was common in the models but also what was different.

8.4 COMPROMISE AND CONSENSUS

The Shared Model activity includes elements of compromise and consensus. Each individual doesn't get all that they want, but can the group come to something they are happy with?

Most groups can. A very small number of groups can't. There is always potential that the Shared Model activity will not work. It's very rare, but it can happen. In seven years, across hundreds and hundreds of sessions, I've had it happen twice.

Here's how to mitigate that risk:

If you think the group might struggle with this type of activity, choose a different one. In the next chapter, I talk about the Landscape Model activity. It is a great activity to use instead of the Shared Model when you have a tricky group.

What are the warning signs that the Shared Model activity might not be the right activity for the group?

- If you have someone extremely dominating in the group. This was the case both times it failed for me.
- If you have people who you know will struggle to let go of their ideas and incorporate other views.

You also might be thinking, 'Why do a Shared Model if there is the potential to fail?' Because there is power in it. The conversation is more challenging, but from that, you can get deeper insights.

A Shared Model activity should have a certain amount of creative friction; that's where the good insights come from. But having way too much friction can jeopardise the process. Unfortunately, I can't draw that clear line for you in a book: there are too many variables and it's too context dependent. But with experience, you'll start to see how far you can push the group to get that creative friction.

I do a lot of Shared Models because the activity achieves certain outcomes better than anything else in LSP. When you want the group to commit, when you want the group to have ownership, when you want one shared understanding of something, the Shared Model activity is very powerful.

8.5 GALLERY

Below are examples of Shared Models and their stories. For each of these, I ran the normal Individual Model activity and then used those models to run a Shared Model activity, exactly as I described above in section 8.2. The stories you'll read are, again, just highlights of a more detailed story that the group told at the time.

SHARED MODEL 1

'What are we good at? What do we want to be known for? Where are our areas for innovation?'

These were some of the Individual Model questions I asked on our way to a Shared Model for a HR consultancy. It represents their current state, the journey they

Shared Model 1: A Shared Model from a company strategy workshop.

are taking and the vision of what they want to see in the future.

It starts at the net in the back on the right where they have captured a shark. This represents their blind spots and working hard to identify them and overcome them.

The garden at the back near the net represents:

> *Our diverse offering. It's a little scattered and unclear to others. We know there are a lot of good things in there, good elements we can offer to people. The garden is our own backyard. Keeping it tidy and as smooth flowing as we can. We're navigating through that using all these eyes. Looking out, looking in. So we can take the client and ourselves over the bridge to the next stage.*

The blue, transparent structure in the middle is what they are building now in terms of services. 'Here we have a clear vision. We have the big idea for the clients on top (the blue globe). We're also side by side with the elephant client who is still slow moving but much stronger now.

The other element is the team up on the platform. They're celebrating and enjoying what they're doing and are supporting the base of that big idea on top.

There were a lot of other interesting aspects to the model and story, including discussions around what workplace culture they wanted and how they were seen as a company from the outside. One interesting saying that came up in the session was 'Whatever we build, it must be transparent to all'. That was in response to the diverse, eclectic offerings the company currently have. In the future, they want to make sure everyone (themselves, partner companies and clients) have a clear view of those offerings and how they fit together.

SHARED MODEL 2

'Who are we at our core? Who do we want to be?'

These were two Individual Model questions I asked on our way to a Shared Model for an innovation team at a local government department.

Shared Model 2: Part of a Shared Model from a team identity session. This shows the current state of the wider organisation.

This team built their Shared Model as a four-quadrant model. The quadrants were (1) the current state of the organisation, (2) the current state of our team, (3) the future state of the organisation and (4) the future state of our team.

The photo above shows the current state of the organisation:

> *We have a bunch of people with outdated services and processes kind of walking around like zombies. We have a couple of slow animals who want to sit*

Shared Model 2: Part of a Shared Model from a team identity session. This shows the current state of the team.

> *and eat this little grass because that's just the world they know. Even though there is a potential future state that is a whole lot more delicious. But that's just where they are in the world currently.*

The photo above shows where the team are at right now:

> *In terms of our team, we have a whole bunch of people who are kind of working together. It's a little bit disjointed at the moment. It's a bit of a rocky stage that we're all in, but still functioning together. And*

Shared Model 2: Part of a Shared Model from a team identity session. This shows one aspect of how the team are currently feeling.

> *we have a cool little guy who has been chopped in half'* (see photo above).
>
> *We're split a little bit between the team and the organisation. We're being pulled in two different directions.*

You can also see, over the last three photos, a big blue LEGO plate standing vertically between the team and the organisation.

> *There is also this big wall between us and the organisation which is co-constructed at the moment. The*

Shared Model 2: Part of a Shared Model from a team identity session. This shows the vision for the team and the wider organisation.

black bricks at the base are the organisation's fear of change.

Here's our future team state (top left, colourful bricks and Minifigures on a blue base). We're a really nice, cohesive team with clear service offerings to the organisation, with a really clear set of roles. We're wearing multiple hats and we have lots of different people with lots of different outfits and skills.

Here we have the future state of the organisation (foreground, middle and right). A lot of looking out to work out what's happening in the world (eyes in the foreground).

We've got a lot of people who are engaged and empowered to design their own destiny. We provide the organisation the safety net so they feel safe in their move towards a future state. We put the safety net in front of the people rather than behind. Originally, we were going to put it behind the figures. But we chose to put it in front because we felt that if you put the safety net behind, people are going to use that as a fallback and go backwards. We want them to feel safe to move forward. So, we need to work out how to build a safety net in front of people, not behind them.

There are lots of opportunities. Each blue sphere is a different opportunity to explore as an organisation. They have different things inside them. Some good things but also potentially some bombs. We don't know what's in them, but the organisation should feel safe to explore them.

SHARED MODEL 3

'It's two years into the future. Your team are recognised as the most successful in the industry. How did you do it? What has made you so successful?'

This Shared Model is from a multinational public relations and marketing company. The question I asked is a little trick you can do to get people to think differently

Shared Model 3: A Shared Model from a team vision workshop.

about the future. Instead of asking what you want in the future, you can put people into a future where they're already successful and ask them to look around! What do they notice? What made them successful? This mindset shift helps the group to bypass any immediate roadblocks they have in the present and leap into a desired future.

> *This treasure chest represents a lot of things. It's not to do with money. It's harmony. It's equality. It's all of the values that we live by. It's all in there.*
>
> *All these people are coming from every aspect of life. Every journey, every culture, every race,*

everything that they entail. We respect that and take it on board. These bricks (next to each person) are what they bring to the table, their contributions. That ensures that we are the most successful team. Everyone's opinion counts. We learn from each other and feel more rewarded and more enriched from the experience we've gained from other people.

SHARED MODEL 4

'Who are we at our core? What is our internal, external and aspirational identity?'

Again, a series of Individual Model questions that lead to a Shared Model of a vision for a medium-sized product management consultancy.

It starts from the right and shows the path that customers take when they engage with this company.

The green baseplate represents the start outside of our company. Customers come to us for our knowledge and our understanding. To come into our world and start to take a journey with us. Up the stairs we introduce to them the processes and frameworks that they need (the yellow flower and column). That can be a difficult challenge for them, sometimes people see that as being a hard point to get to.

Shared Model 4: A Shared Model from a team strategy session.

The middle (beige) baseplate occurs within our company. The help we give people. We have this bridge over the mess, the mess is product management and all the blockers out there. We have lots of different customers. Some come to us the traditional way from the start up the stairs. Some are down in this mess and we have a rope to rescue them.

The blue baseplate is people taking their new ideas to the outside world. Building off the framework they have learnt. Raised up on a column to become superstar product managers, recognised by their peers and clients.

Shared Model 4: A movable part of a Shared Model from a team identity session.

Then you have the courageous people (represented by the lion) who come back around and share these learnings with the people back at the start. (In the actual model the lion moved from the end back to the start.) *They may be bringing their own team with them or helping and mentoring others.*

8.6 LAST THOUGHTS ON SHARED MODELS

What's interesting from all these examples of Shared Models is that I only scratched the surface of the conversations that took place. For each part of these Shared Models, there was a rich discussion on what the elements meant and how they related back to real work.

The fact that it's all laid out visually allows for people to point to different elements and bring them into the conversation when needed. The conversations are much more dynamic, as the whole 'system' is spread out in front of people for them to reference when necessary.

Chapter 9

LANDSCAPE MODELS

In the previous chapter, you saw how a group can take their Individual Models and combine them into one Shared Model, going from an individual view to a group perspective.

In this chapter, you'll learn another group activity that brings those Individual Models together, but in a different way. It's called a Landscape Model.

9.1 LANDSCAPE MODEL OVERVIEW

A Landscape Model is when a group take their Individual Models, keep them intact and arrange them on the table to show relationships using space. Every aspect of where the models are placed has meaning. How far from or close to other models they are, which way they face and how they are grouped are all important.

Think of the Individual Models as separate, distinct ideas in model form. A Landscape Model helps the group to bring order to all those ideas, using where they are placed on the table to show the relationships *between* the ideas.

From this simple idea of using space and placement to show relationships, you get an incredibly flexible activity. Sometimes a landscape has an overarching story to it. This model happens first, then this model happens, then the next one. Or sometimes the landscape has groupings of different models, with similar ideas or models grouped together and different models placed further away. The Landscape Model activity can play out in many ways.

Here are just a handful of examples of how you can use this activity:

- **Innovation**. What is the key element for successful innovation at our company? Get each participant to build that as an Individual Model. Then, have the group place those models into a landscape showing a successful innovation journey.
- **Risks**. What are the risks our project is facing? Get each participant to build that as an Individual Model. Then have the group place those models into a landscape showing groupings of risks.
- **Team Culture**. What are the aspects of team life you feel are important over the next year? Get

each participant to build that as an Individual Model. Then have the group place those models into a landscape. The landscape could end up as groupings of similar ideas or could have a story element, or even both groupings and a story.

At the end of the Landscape Model activity, when the group have placed all their models on the table, they have essentially created a sweeping landscape of ideas and how they are related to each other.

9.2 LANDSCAPE MODEL STEPS

To facilitate a Landscape Model, first get the group to build Individual Models. Take the group through the standard Individual Model activity (Question, Build, Share, Capture).

There is a slight twist here, depending on how you want your upcoming landscape to take shape. Normally in the Individual Model activity each person takes five minutes and builds only one model. It's perfectly fine to do that here and then go on to build the Landscape Model.

But for some landscapes you might want each person to build more than one model. For example, you could ask 'What is a challenge facing the team?' Get each person to spend three minutes building an Individual Model.

Before they share their model, get them to put it to the side and build another Individual Model representing a different challenge the team faces. After the two models are built, each person can then share their stories.

Now when you come to build the Landscape Model, you have twice as many models. For some questions, this idea of building multiple Individual Models makes for a richer landscape.

The choice you have here as facilitator is to get each participant to build either one, two or three Individual Models. That choice depends a lot on how much time you have, the size of the group, the type of question you ask, whether you're looking for quality or quantity and how big you want your landscape to be. There's no one right answer.

As an example, for a group of six people, I would look to do two models each, for a total of twelve models to put into the landscape. That provides a nice balance between having enough models or ideas for an interesting landscape, but not so many as to be overwhelming. But again, that could vary depending on the type of question I'm asking.

Once all the Individual Models are built and the stories shared, then the group are ready to place those models into the landscape.

Overall, your role in facilitating the Landscape Model activity is very similar to the role you played in the last chapter for the Shared Model activity.

STEP 1: QUESTION

The group have finished the Individual Model build. They've shared their stories; they've reflected; they've captured. They have their models on the table in front of them.

Guide them by saying the following:

You have all built Individual Models showing [insert your topic]. Now it's time to bring them together to see if any themes emerge. To do that, we're going to build what's called a landscape. Think of the table top as a vast landscape, and soon you will place your models into that landscape to show the relationships between the models.

Where you position your model, the distance it is from other models and the direction it is facing all have meaning. For example, I can place this model here, close to another model and facing towards it. That's very different to placing it further away, facing outward.

There are only two rules: (1) each model must remain intact and (2) the models should have some space between each other. Otherwise the landscape gets too crowded and it's hard to see any themes.

Again, this activity is about placing your models into

the landscape to show how they relate to each other. You're forming a landscape of [insert your topic].

For the Landscape Model activity, there is no need for a baseplate. The table itself becomes the space where models are placed.

There's no time limit for this activity. It normally takes around fifteen to thirty minutes, depending on the topic and number of models.

STEP 2: BUILD

This step is less about building and more about placing models.

You, as facilitator, can structure this step in two different ways:

1. **Freeform Discussion**. The group can have a freeform discussion about where things fit. In this version, conversation moves freely from person to person with people jumping in and placing models into the landscape when they want. This allows the discussion (and landscape) to evolve organically.
2. **Rounds**. This is a more structured approach in which each person takes a turn and places one of their models into the landscape. It's

up to the person who built the model to decide where it goes. The rest of the group can offer advice. Once everyone has placed their first model, the group can then do another round until all the models are placed in the landscape.

The decision of which approach to use depends on the type of group you have.

The freeform discussion is my preferred option. It leads to more interesting connections and stories. But it does open up the space for someone to dominate the conversation. If you think that could be a problem with your group, try doing this step in rounds instead.

Once all the models have been placed in the landscape, it's important to shift your focus to refining the landscape. You can use all the same tricks that we discussed in chapter 8: Devil's Advocate, Personas, Quiet Time, Move Around.

If you have time, another way to refine the Landscape Model is to encourage people to try their models in a different spot. 'If you were going to place your model in a different spot, where would it be? Try it out.' It's easy enough to go back to the original landscape.

Once the landscape is refined and the group are happy with the model, move on to Share and Capture.

STEPS 3 AND 4: SHARE AND CAPTURE

Your role is the same as outlined for the Shared Model activity.

Get the group as a whole to tell the story of the landscape, highlighting any themes that emerge. People can jump in at different points to provide more details.[4]

I also like to capture or record the story as a video on my phone. The video is a great resource to use after the session to pull out themes and quotes to help remind the group of the insights they had.

After the story of the Landscape Model has been told, wrap up this activity with the usual reflection questions:

- 'What did you see and hear in that activity?'
- 'Are there any themes emerging?'
- 'What were the key insights for you?'

9.3 GALLERY

Below are examples of Landscape Models. For each of these, I ran the normal Individual Model activity (usually getting each person to build two models) and

4 For bigger groups where you have multiple tables doing landscapes, follow the same process as described in 8.3—Multiple Tables in the last chapter when sharing between tables.

then I used the resulting models to run a Landscape Model activity.

I haven't included in-depth stories for each model. The purpose of the gallery is to show you what Landscape Models look like. But know that each landscape (and, indeed, each Individual Model within the landscape) has a rich story behind it.

LANDSCAPE MODEL 1

'What is one key element that helps drive innovation in an organisation?'

I got this group to build two quicker models each and lay them out in a landscape. You can see in this model

Landscape Model 1: A Landscape Model on innovation.

Landscape Model 1. TOP: : Often, the table itself works its way into the story! BOTTOM: I particularly liked this model of 'staying in a vision bubble to get over barriers.'

that the group chose a circular pattern for their landscape, in order to show how one thing leads on to the next and the whole story loops back around to the start.

LANDSCAPE MODEL 2

'What is one key element that helps drive innovation in an organisation?'

I posed the same question as in the last example and again I got the group to build two quicker models each. This group chose a more linear pattern for their model.

Landscape Model 2: A Landscape Model on innovation.

TOP: : Landscape Model 2: The reverse angle of a Landscape Model on innovation. BOTTOM: Landscape Model 3: A Landscape Model showing the opportunities and challenges of a company.

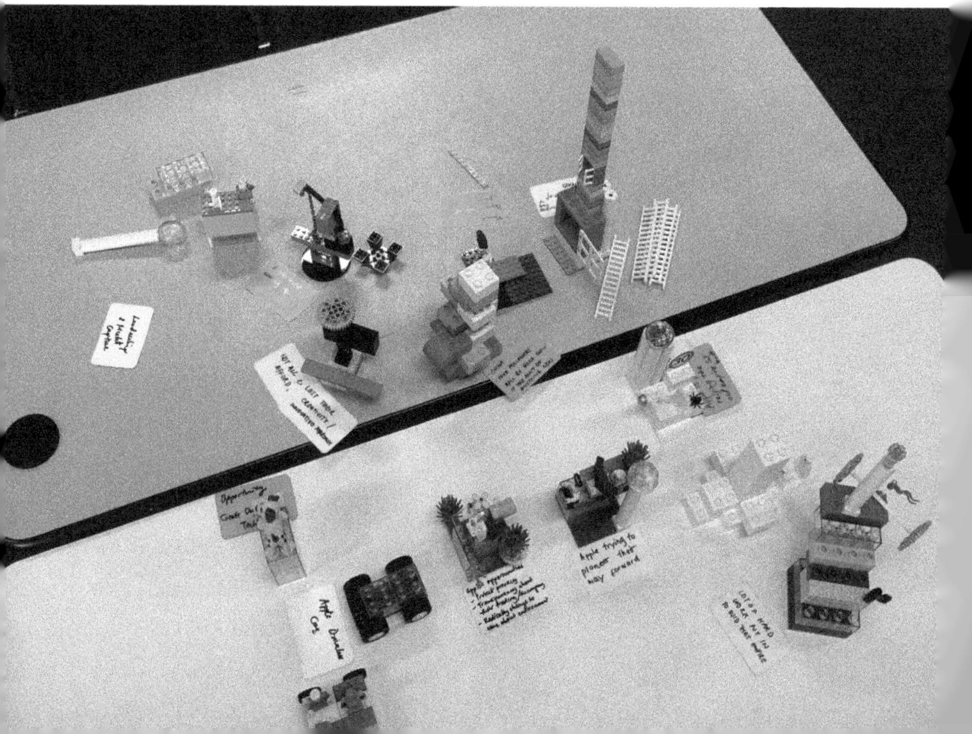

LANDSCAPE MODEL 3

'What are the opportunities facing your chosen company? What are the challenges facing your chosen company?'

This was from a session with students at an education company called General Assembly. The students were mid-career and were undertaking an intensive twelve-week full-time course to reskill in the user- or customer-experience field.

These questions were part of a case study they were doing in which they would choose a company and assess its opportunities and challenges. I got each person to build one Individual Model for an opportunity and then build another Individual Model for a challenge. They then placed both models into a landscape.

In the photo opposite, the challenges were in a line on the top table, starting from the right and going left. The opportunities were on the bottom table, again going from right to left.

Laying out the models in this visual manner led to an interesting discussion about where the challenges and opportunities interrelated.

9.4 LAST THOUGHTS ON LANDSCAPE MODELS

What I find interesting about the Landscape Model activity is that you maintain the richness from all the original Individual Models, but by placing them in a landscape, you see their interrelationship.

For example, the 'vision bubble' model from above had a rich story behind it, and then we saw how and where it 'fit in' with other ideas.

That's the real power of the Landscape Model activity. It doesn't always integrate the ideas as tightly as a Shared Model but it maintains richness and shows relationships.

9.5 SHARED MODELS VERSUS LANDSCAPE MODELS

Shared Models and Landscape Models have a lot of similarities in the way they are facilitated and what they achieve. When learning LSP for the first time, it can be confusing to decide which of these two activities to run. Here are some ways in which the activities are different and some principles that help me decide which one to use.

SHARED MODEL

- Break up and recombine Individual Models
- Use a baseplate
- Total time: thirty to forty minutes

The Shared Model is a more challenging activity, from a group dynamics perspective, because it requires each person to break up their model and integrate it tightly with other models or ideas. It involves compromise, finding consensus and putting one's ego to the side. Psychologically, this is harder to do than a Landscape Model, so you will see a wider range of group dynamics playing out. Most of the time it is fine, but there is the potential for more disruptions, so you need to be on watch as a facilitator.

LANDSCAPE MODEL

- Models remain intact
- The table is the landscape
- Total time: fifteen to thirty minutes

The Landscape Model is a less challenging activity, from a group dynamics perspective, because the models remain intact. Each person can still see the entirety of their idea right there on the table; they don't lose anything or have to integrate their ideas as tightly with others as compared to a Shared Model. There still is, and needs to be, some group friction to help synthesise the ideas and come up with new insights. But, from a facilitator perspective, it is an easier activity to run.

HOW TO DECIDE BETWEEN SHARED AND LANDSCAPE

There's no hard and fast rule about when to use a Shared Model or a Landscape Model. But here are some principles that help:

- If you want everyone to commit to one solution (e.g., strategy, a vision, team culture), do a Shared Model.
- If you have a range of answers and want to maintain their integrity (e.g., challenges, benefits, stakeholders), do a Landscape.
- If you are short on time, a Landscape is quicker.
- If you have a group that you think might struggle with compromise and consensus, do a Landscape.
- If you want to go deeper into a topic, do a Shared Model.

While I've presented the Shared Model and Landscape Model activities as separate, they're not that different. I've had plenty of Shared Models that have spread out like a Landscape. I've had plenty of Landscapes that look like a Shared Model.

I always teach them as two separate activities. When I'm designing sessions, I think of them as separate activities. When I'm describing them to participants, I do them as separate activities. But deep down, there is a lot of overlap in these activities.

As you run them more, you'll get a better feel for what each activity is capable of.

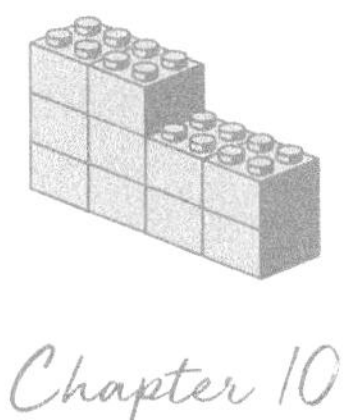

Chapter 10

OTHER ACTIVITIES

Over the last three chapters, you've learnt the three main activities to use in an LSP session (Individual, Shared, Landscape). Those activities are flexible enough to tackle almost any topic.

A LEGO Serious Play session can be any combination of these activities. You could get the group to build Individual Models and then stop. That would be a perfectly fine LSP session. You could get the group to build some Individual Models, build them into a Shared Model and then stop. You could get the group to build Individual Models, then a Landscape Model and then stop.

Don't feel that you need to pack your LSP sessions with all the activities you know.

That's particularly important as we go through this chapter. You'll be introduced to a couple of other activities that build on top of what you already know. But think of them as additions to your toolkit that you can pull out and use if they fit the objective you're trying to achieve.

10.1 SHARED MODEL + LANDSCAPE MODEL

This first activity is nothing new to you, and in fact, it's not really an activity by itself. It is simply the layering of the three activities you already know: the Individual Model, the Shared Model and the Landscape Model. This layering creates an interesting effect on how the group see a topic.

The aim of this set of activities is to build a Shared Model in the middle and then build a Landscape Model around it.

Why would you want to do this? It works really well when you want the group to come to a common understanding of a topic (the Shared Model in the middle) and then to map out the broader ecosystem that sits *around* the topic (the Landscape Model).

The most common use case of this activity is when a group build their team strategy as a Shared Model (going through all the normal steps we talked about in chapter 8). Then the group build all the Agents that impact the team as Individual Models and then place those Agent models in the Landscape around the Shared Model.

A Landscape Model around a Shared Model.

In this way, you see both the team strategy in the middle (Shared Model) and what influences it (the Agents in the Landscape).

A lengthy aside: you might be wondering, 'What's an Agent?' It's a special term used in LSP and comes from the original LSP Strategy Workshop developed in the early 2000s. An Agent is anything that has an impact or influence on a system. It can be a stakeholder; a broader trend; an event; something cultural, economic or technical; or anything tangible or even intangible that has a significant impact.

Examples of Agents affecting a company strategy (for example) can include:

- Government (stakeholder)
- Big competitors (stakeholder)
- Economic trade war (event)
- Pandemic (event)
- Rise of mobile and online (trend)
- Increasing speed of change (intangible)

Anything can be an Agent, depending on the topic. The key is to identify the important Agents that are having an impact on your topic. The next photo shows

An Agent model showing a big market leader. It's placed in a Landscape around a Shared Model.

the Agent 'big market leaders' and is quite appropriately built as an elephant with a prize cup and a gun on top (aimed at the Shared Model of this particular company).

The idea of placing Agents as models in the Landscape around the Shared Model is just one example of how you can use this Shared Model + Landscape Model activity. The group can tackle many other topics using this type of activity:

- 'Problem or challenge' as the Shared Model. 'Solutions' as the surrounding Landscape.
- 'Shared understanding or vision for a project' as the Shared Model. 'Benefits and risks' as the surrounding Landscape.
- 'Value proposition' as the Shared Model. 'Customer segments' as the surrounding Landscape.
- 'Team vision' as the Shared Model. 'Enablers and inhibitors' as the surrounding Landscape.

Again, the pattern to this activity is the common understanding of a topic in the middle and then a range of models around the outside. They could be Agents, challenges, risks, enablers, customers, solutions or anything you want the group to build!

STEPS

Here are the specific steps to run this activity (we're going to use a team vision session as an example):

1. **Individual Models.** Run a standard Individual Model activity as described in chapter 7. For this example, the question would be 'What is your vision for the team over the next two years?'
2. **Shared Model.** Run a standard Shared Model activity as described in chapter 8. For this example, the question would be 'Combine your models into one Shared Model showing what the vision is for our team over the next two years'. Once the group have finished building the Shared Model, put it off to the side and continue on.
3. **Individual Models.** Run a standard Individual Model activity as described in chapter 7. For this example, the question would be 'What is one key Agent that is influencing us as a team and our ability to achieve that vision?' (Three-minute build.) Get the group to put those models to the side and then get each of them to build again: 'What is another key Agent influencing us as a team and our ability to achieve that vision?' (Three-minute build.)

4. **Landscape Model.** Run a standard Landscape Model activity as described in chapter 9, except that you will get the group to place their previously built Individual Agent Models around the Shared Model. Guide them by saying 'Place your Agent models into the Landscape around the Shared Model. Where you place your model is important. Which part of the Shared Model does the Agent relate to? How close to or far away from the Shared Model should it be? Which other Agents should it be near?'

At the end of this sequence of activities, you have a set of models showing a shared understanding of the topic and the landscape or ecosystem around it that influences it.

10.2 CONNECTIONS

Remember that, in the Landscape Model activity, space and placement are used to show relationships between models.

This next activity, the Connections activity, takes that a step further and uses a physical LEGO connector to show relationships between models.

This activity is most commonly used after the Shared Model + Landscape Model activity. The group have built a Shared Model and have placed some models in a Landscape around it. The group then attach connectors between models to show other relationships.

The photo to the right shows a team strategy as a Shared Model in the middle. Agents affecting the team have been placed in the Landscape around the Shared Model and then a set of connectors has been used to show other relationships between models.

Why use connectors to show even more relationships? Using just space to show relationships (like in a Landscape Model) has limitations. For example, 'These two models are next to each other, but they also have a relationship to a model way over on the other side of the table. How do I show all those complex relationships using just space and placement?' That's where connectors can help.

Another example is 'This model is close to this part of the Shared Model, but the real relationship is from this one little brick on my model to one specific part of that Shared Model. How do I show that level of detail with just space and placement?' Connectors allow you to get really specific with how you show relationships.

As I mentioned, the most common use of Connections is after the Shared Model + Landscape Model activity. But you can use Connections with any other activity. Two Individual Models? Put a connector between them. A landscape of ideas? Throw some connectors in there.

A Landscape Model around a Shared Model with Connections. This was for a university innovation team.

STEPS

Here are the specific steps for how you, as facilitator, run this activity. We're going to use the Shared Model + Landscape Model example:

1. Get the group to build a Shared Model and then Individual Models of Agents. Place the Agents in the landscape around the Shared Model.
2. Lay out a range of LEGO connectors. There is a specific Connections kit, but it's expensive

and has way too many pieces. You can find some simple LEGO connectors in other kits or purchase them individually from LEGO or BrickLink. You can even use non-LEGO material (e.g., string) if you want. Another option is to do your building on top of white flip chart paper. Then you can draw the connections between models.

3. Guide the group by saying, 'Each of you choose one model in the landscape (in this example, an Agent) and connect it to the Shared Model using a connector. Your choice of connector has meaning. What type of connection is it? Fixed, flexible, straight, indirect? Choose the connector that best represents that relationship.' Allow everyone to do this at the same time. You may need to provide some technical LEGO assistance to help some people make the connections.
4. After all the connectors have been placed, go around the table and ask each person to spend thirty seconds telling the group which connection they did and why (including the type of connector used).
5. Repeat steps 3 and 4, but this time, ask each person to make a connection between two

models in the landscape (in this example, between two Agents). Two rounds of connections are usually enough. More than that and it gets a bit like spaghetti.

One variation of the Connections activity you might find useful is, instead of getting each person to make a connection, give the group only three connectors (or pieces of string) and let them discuss as a group which are the three most important connections they would like to highlight.

Remember that the Connections activity can be used with any other activity. It doesn't have to come at the end of a long chain of activities as in the example I've used.

Another example of a Landscape Model around a Shared Model with Connections.

10.3 YOUR LSP TOOLKIT

That concludes the main LSP activities. Your sessions will consist of some combination of:

- Individual
- Shared
- Landscape
- Shared + Landscape
- Connections

For some context, most of my sessions use only those three main activities (Individual, Shared and Landscape). I sometimes get to a Shared + Landscape. I rarely get to the Connections activity (mostly because of time and the type of sessions I do). But it's good to know you have all these activities in your toolkit should the objective need it and the time permit it.

10.4 NON-LEGO ACTIVITIES

Now that the group have built these wonderful LSP models and had some great conversations and insights, you can either:

- Go straight to the final activity in the next chapter and crystallise those insights into action
  or

- Run some non-LEGO activities to dive even deeper and generate more insights

Most of my sessions go straight to the final activity. I rarely use any non-LEGO activities. This is partially due to time, but also because I often achieve my objective with just the main LSP activities. But for other facilitators, the LSP models are a useful tool for further activities and conversations.

Scenarios is a popular activity in which the group play out potential scenarios using the LSP models created. Create a scenario (or let the group create a scenario), describe it to the group and then ask them, 'If this scenario happened, what would be the impact on the models?' After a discussion, ask, 'If this scenario happened, how would we as a group respond?' From the ensuing discussion, the group can gain more valuable insights on how the models and the team react in real time to a changing environment.

Scenarios is just one activity you could do with the group. Feel free to use any other non-LEGO activity here that will get you closer to your objective. But feel equally free to do as I do and skip straight to the final activity.

Chapter 11

FINAL ACTIVITY

The group have done the intro and Skills Building. You've taken them through some Individual Models. Maybe you had them build a Shared or Landscape Model and possibly even used some other activities. All of this has generated different thinking, which has led to different conversations. People have reflected on that and have gained some new insights.

Now what? How do you wrap this thing up?

The LSP method is so flexible and is used in such a wide variety of cases that there is no set way to end a session. You can end a LEGO Serious Play session any way you want!

I'll show you my favourite ways to end a session and briefly mention some other options. But remember, the overriding message is to end your session in whatever way helps you achieve your objective.

11.1 WHY THE FINAL ACTIVITY IS IMPORTANT

No matter what the topic is, making *change* happen is at the foundation of everything we do. Whether it's individual behaviour, the direction of a team or company, or the outcome of a project, our aim is change.

The reason we gather together and use LEGO Serious Play is to increase our chances of change happening.

Change is hard, whether at the personal, team or organisational level. Meetings and workshops can be one of the primary sparks of that change. But we've all experienced having a good meeting or workshop, walking out of the room and nothing changes. No real action. No real change.

Your role in ending an LSP session is to help people take those good insights and convert them into change in the real world.

11.2 WHAT DO YOU NORMALLY DO?

The first option to explore when looking to end your LSP sessions is 'what you normally do to end your meetings'.

Many people ask me, 'What's the output from a LEGO Serious Play session?'

I reply, 'What would you normally do to end a meeting or workshop?' They usually say the participants would generate a set of actions to take or would gain a better understanding of a topic.

'Well, the output from LSP can be just that. What you would normally do, but better.'

Think of LSP not as an output, but rather as a tool to help the processing of inputs. It's like a Post-it note or a whiteboard. There's no special output from a whiteboard. It's a tool that helps you visualise something, with the end result being a better outcome.

Look to 'what you normally do' as a potential way to run your final activity and end your LSP sessions. The format of that output might look the same as normal, but by using LSP the quality of that output is improved.

11.3 FINISH WITH ACTIONS

My favourite way to end a session is with *actions*. Individuals and teams should walk out of a session knowing exactly what they need to do to progress the topic or issue.

I like to use a method called ORID as my final activity. It's general enough to apply to most of my sessions and it helps bring accountability for change right down to the individual level.

ORID

You'll remember that throughout I've used a series of debrief questions to help groups reflect on their experience:

- What did you see and hear?
- What were your key insights?

These questions are part of a broader framework called ORID. It's an acronym in which each letter stands for a type of question to ask the group:

- O: **Objective** questions explore the reality of the experience ('What did you see and hear?')
- R: **Reflective** questions dive into the emotional aspect ('How did that make you feel?')
- I: **Interpretive** questions help us find the meaning of the experience. ('What were your key insights?')
- D: **Decisional** questions encourage us to take the action we want. ('What action will you take?')

After all the LEGO activities, I finish my LSP sessions by going through the full ORID (in a discussion style, not through building any models):

- Ask the Objective question to the entire group: 'What did you see and hear throughout this session?' A couple of people will give you their responses, and from that, you can have an open, facilitated discussion with the whole group. Feel free to include any themes you noticed that weren't picked up by the group.

- Repeat this for the Reflective question: 'How did that make you feel?'
- Have each person get out an index card and ask the group the Interpretive question: 'What was your key insight from today's session?' The twist here is that this is done individually, not as a group. You get each person to write down their key insight on an index card in silence.
- After that, ask each person to take out another index card and ask them the Decisional question. You could ask the normal question: 'What action will you take?' But I like to use an alternative wording that gets better results: 'What action can you do right now without needing more resources or authority? Where do you have discretion and freedom to act?[5] What action will you take, no matter how small?' The

5 This little twist of the wording of the question is from Liberating Structures, developed by Henri Lipmanowicz and Keith McCandless, and inspired by professor Gareth Morgan.

reason I use this alternative wording is because some people like to write down very high-level actions like 'I'll collaborate more'. Bringing it back to what each person has control over helps to make the actions more specific and meaningful.

- If you have time, get people into pairs to share their actions and get feedback from the other person. Give them a moment to refine their action and then move on to the next step. If you're short on time, skip the pairs and go straight to the next step.
- After writing insights and actions, get each person to share with the entire group what they wrote down. Speaking it aloud to the group heightens the commitment they've made.

The ORID final activity is quick, structured and covers the important steps of helping the group to process the session and take action.

It is very individual, though, which can help people take ownership of their actions. But it means you do end up with a lot of uncoordinated actions happening.

For some topics or conversations, a more coordinated team approach might be better. In that case, you can go one step further by putting those individual actions up on a board and getting the group to prioritise them into a team plan (see below, where I discuss Kanban boards).

Whether people leave with individual actions or a team plan, the ORID activity is a great way to wrap up an LSP session and help change happen.

11.4 FINISH WITH SOMETHING TANGIBLE

'What do you normally do?' and ORID are my two favourite ways to end a session.

But here are two other ways that you might find useful. They both involve creating something tangible, something physical for the group to take out of the room.

The advantage of doing this is that it takes a little bit of that magic that was created in the session and transfers it out of the room and into the normal world, with the aim of helping change to occur.

LEGO MODEL

As a final activity, you could get each participant to do an Individual Model where they build the action they are going to take. It would be as simple as running through the standard four steps (Question, Build, Share, Capture). At the end, people can take their models back to their desks and have a physical reminder of what they committed to.

It's powerful, it works, but here is why I don't do it:

- For an external consultant like me, leaving the LEGO with each client is a big additional cost. I would also need to keep renewing my kits, which is a pain.
- Doing an extra Individual Model build takes up more time in the workshop.
- Lastly, I like the idea of converting the insights from a session into something that more naturally fits into the workplace (pen and paper).

Between the extra cost, extra hassle and the extra time, I've decided to do the ORID final activity instead.

If you're using LSP internally within an organisation, then you can avoid some of these problems by getting the models back off people before the next session.

Building an LSP model as the final activity is an option that I encourage you to explore. However, I personally don't finish my sessions with an LSP build.

KANBAN BOARDS

Another way to create something tangible for the group to take away is with Kanban boards.

They are a physical workflow tool that's used in the IT/agile world. The board helps teams track tasks as they go from idea through to implementation.

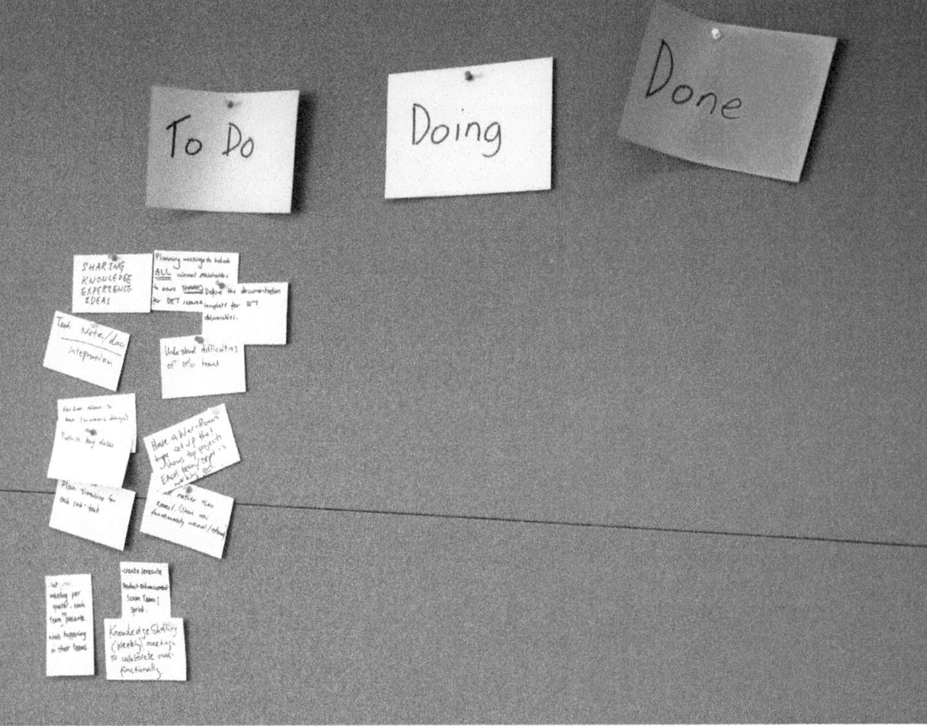

This was one of the first Kanban Boards I did after an LSP session. They don't need to be fancy: a couple of bits of paper and some index cards will do the trick!

A basic Kanban board can help teams make change happen. Here are the key features:

- There are three columns: To Do, Doing, Done.
- Each task or action is on a separate index card.
- A card starts in the To Do column. Someone picks up that bit of work and moves the card to the Doing column. When they complete it, it gets moved to the Done column. Simple!
- Each individual limits their 'work in progress' to one card only, focusing on that task or card and

only starting another one when they have finished the previous one.
- The board should be placed somewhere everyone can see it.

Note that this is not a general board where the team put all their day-to-day work. In our context, it's a special board just for the topic the team discussed in the LSP session.

The team can have it up in their work area and track the progress of the action items coming out of the LSP session. They can also keep filling up the To Do column with new ideas days and weeks afterwards. These new ideas may come from doing the work and having further insights or from other meetings or workshops. In this way, the board becomes a living tool, evolving over the weeks as work gets done and new ideas are added.

There are lots of advantages to this type of board: It's physical. It's visual. It shows people at a glance what you're working on.

I'm exploring the use of Kanban boards in that moment straight after you've run the ORID activity and you want to bring the actions together as a team. The team collect all the actions and put them into the To Do column, prioritise them, assign them amongst themselves and then take the Kanban board back to the work area and put it up for everyone to see.

If your team already know about Kanban boards or they are looking to work in a more agile way, this activity is another great way to end an LSP session.

LSP is a great tool to make people speak their minds and to align as a group. But you need to combine it with other tools to make it actionable. Seeing LSP as part of a bigger process helps you to think creatively about wrap-up, follow-up and integration techniques. One technique we use is asking participants to write a letter to their future self with specific commitments.

—Anders and Bjorn

11.5 LAST THOUGHTS ON THE FINAL ACTIVITY

Final activities are important in order to bring together insights and create meaningful actions. The high-level advice is to end your session in whatever way helps you achieve your objective.

Some of my favourite ways are:

1. What do you normally do?
2. ORID
3. LEGO model
4. Kanban board

While many parts of the LSP method have been tested and refined over many years, the final activity is still a space for experimentation and innovation. There will never be one best way to end a session; sessions are too diverse. But we are moving towards a wonderful set of options that allow facilitators to help shape the change we're looking for.

Part III

CUSTOMISE

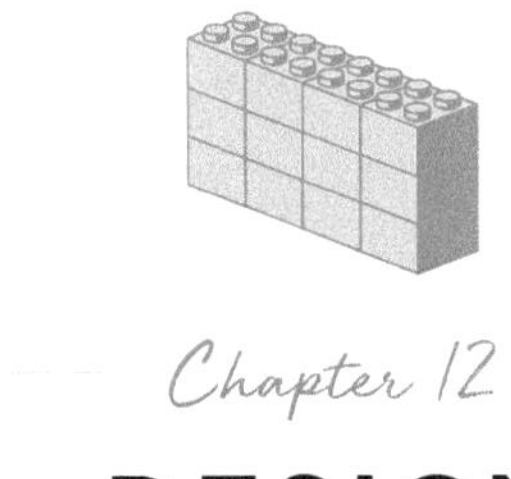

Chapter 12

DESIGN

You now have all the building blocks you need to design your LSP session:

- Introduction
- Skills Building
- Individual Models
- Shared Models
- Landscape Models
- Other activities
- Final activity

Back in chapter 4, we started to discuss when to use LSP and how to design an LSP session. Now that you know the method, let's pick those conversations back up.

12.1 IS LSP THE RIGHT TOOL?

Remember that LSP works well when:

- The topic is complex
- There is no one right answer
- You want everyone's input and engagement

Also remember that LSP can be used for a wide range of topics, including:

- Strategy
- Team identity
- Innovation
- Culture
- Change management
- Team collaboration
- Design thinking
- Job interviews
- Coaching
- Project kick-off meetings
- Retrospectives
- Customer experience
- And many more

At its core, LEGO Serious Play is a tool to help answer questions. All the topics above ask interesting questions:

- What's our strategic direction?
- What do we want our team culture to be?
- How can we collaborate better?
- What is our unique value proposition?
- What risks is this project facing?
- How can we better serve our customers?
- What future state are we trying to achieve?

Those questions are normally answered with talking and some Post-it notes. Instead, we can get people to build their answers using LEGO Serious Play. Combining LSP with other topics and methods is a fantastic way to use the power of LSP to help the work you're already doing.

So, clearly, there are a lot of places where you could use LSP. But it's important to always ask yourself, 'Is LSP the right tool?'

Challenge yourself by asking:

- What is my objective? Does using LSP achieve that?
- Is there a better method for this objective?
- How long do I have with the group? Is that enough time for LSP?

The major 'cost' of doing LSP is time. LSP sessions take longer than normal meetings and workshops.

The major 'benefit' of doing LSP is better engagement and taking a deeper dive into the issue for a better outcome.

Sometimes that extra time is an important investment. Sometimes it's not needed to get the job done. As you start to use LSP and see what it is capable of, you'll get better at deciding when LSP is the right tool.

12.2 DESIGN

Once you've chosen to use LSP, it's time to design your session. Your aim is to produce a customised session each time, moulded to fit your exact topic.

> Never use a blueprint for the facilitation of an LSP session. Always tailor-make your sessions considering participant profiles and expected outcomes of the session.
>
> —Elske

Here are the steps to design your sessions:

- Find your key questions
- Design your session outline
- Refine your questions

12.3 KEY QUESTIONS

What are the key questions that will achieve your objective? Here are four ways I find my questions:

- **Brainstorm**. Put LSP out of your mind. Write down a list of questions you want to know the answer to for your topic. They might not be the exact ones you end up using, but it's a great starting point.
- **Ask Your Client**. If you have a client, they're a great source of questions. Ask them, '*What are the key questions you want answered?*' Listen carefully. They'll often give you the questions for your session.
- **Other Frameworks**. As you saw above, many other topics and frameworks ask great questions. For example, there are many tools in the customer experience toolkit that ask great questions—use those. Many coaching frameworks ask great questions—use those. A variety of strategy models have great questions—use those too. And on and on. All these frameworks have great questions that you can steal and use in your LSP sessions.
- **Past Sessions**. Look for key questions from previous workshops. You can see some in the next chapter. Also, as part of the online LSP community, we are developing a 'Question Library': a place to go and borrow questions that have worked for other people.

At this stage, you're getting a feel for what your questions will be. Don't worry if they're not perfect. We'll look at what makes a good LSP question and how to refine these questions later in the chapter.

> Asking the right questions is key! You can nail that by being pure to the intent of the session. In very practical terms, I probe my clients on the actual outputs they need to see from the session and that almost always guides the type of questions I will use in the session.
>
> —Elma

12.4 SESSION OUTLINE

Time to decide which LSP activities to use and in what order.

I've found it easiest to outline a session in thirty-minute blocks.[6] Each block contains one activity. To design your own outlines, create a table and fill it in with activities and questions.

6 This timing assumes five to six people per table. If you have smaller or larger groups on each table, times will vary a little.

Block	Activity	Question	Time
1	Intro and Skills Building	'Build a tower with you in it.'	30 minutes
2	Individual Model		30 minutes
3	Activity		30 minutes
4	Activity		30 minutes
5	Activity		30 minutes
6	Final activity		30 minutes
	Total time		**3 hours**

The first block is always the intro and Skills Building for a first-time group. Run through all the material that we covered in chapters 5 and 6. If the group already know LSP, do the quicker Explain This! activity to warm them up.

The second block is always an Individual Model. LSP always starts with the individual's view.

Decide on what question to ask and how long participants will build. Remember from chapter 7 that my preference is for a five-minute build, but you can play with the timing to achieve different results. Longer builds promote more considered thinking. Shorter builds promote more instinctive thinking.

For the third block, I like to shift to group work and do either a Shared Model or a Landscape Model.

Alternating between Individual Models and Groups Models works well. Too many Individual Models (three or more) in a row can feel repetitive.

Remember that this Shared or Landscape activity is just the bringing together of Individual Models that you built in the previous block. The thirty minutes devoted to this Shared or Landscape activity assumes that you've already built the Individual Models prior and this time is for building and placing and the storytelling that follows.

Keep filling in the blocks based on the objective you want to achieve and the time you have for the session. Remember that you can use any of the activities you've learnt. Mix and match them to achieve your objective.

The last block is always the final activity that best fits your objective.

This thirty-minute-block design process can help you outline any LSP session you want. But there are four outline patterns I've found particularly powerful:

- Individual -> Shared -> final activity
- Individual -> Landscape -> final activity
- Individual -> Shared -> Individual -> Landscape -> final activity
- Individual -> non-LSP content -> Individual

Topics and questions will change depending on the objective. But these patterns can cover a lot of sessions.

Here are some examples that use these four patterns:

PATTERN 1

This type of session starts with an Individual Model build, combines those models into a Shared Model and ends with a final activity. As an example, here is a two-hour team culture session.

Block	Activity	Question	Time
1	Intro and Skills Building	'Build a tower with you in it.'	30 minutes
2	Individual Model	'What do you want our team culture to be in the future?' (5-minute build)	30 minutes
3	Shared Model	'Combine your models into one Shared Model showing what you want our team culture to be.'	30 minutes
4	Final activity	ORID	30 minutes
	Total time		**2 hours**

PATTERN 2

This type of session starts with an Individual Model build (often with multiple, quicker builds). The group takes those models and arranges them into a Landscape Model and then does a final activity. As an example, here is a two-hour customer experience session.

Block	Activity	Question	Time
1	Intro and Skills Building	'Build a tower with you in it.'	30 minutes
2	Individual Model	'How can we improve our customer experience?' (2-minute build x 3)	30 minutes
3	Landscape Model	'Put your models into the centre of the table and place them in relationship to each other to form a Landscape.'	30 minutes
4	Final activity	ORID	30 minutes
	Total time		**2 hours**

These two patterns can be used for almost any topic you want to focus on. For example:

- **Innovation**. 'What drives successful innovation?' Build Individual Models. Combine them into a Shared Model showing best practices in innovation (Pattern 1).

- **Project Risks.** 'What are the potential risks for our project?' Build Individual Models. Instead of a Shared Model, do a Landscape. You now have a Landscape of project risks where themes emerge (Pattern 2).

PATTERN 3

This next pattern is for going deeper into a topic. It layers in more of the surrounding ecosystem, allowing you to see the bigger picture of what is happening. It starts with Individual Model builds. Those are combined into a Shared Model, and then more Individual Models are built (often with multiple, quicker builds) and placed in the Landscape around the Shared Model. It's the exact same Shared + Landscape pattern you saw in chapter 10.

For the example below, I've taken the two-hour team culture workshop and added in the next layer to make it a three-hour session that dives deeper.

Block	Activity	Question	Time
1	Intro and Skills Building	'Build a tower with you in it.'	30 minutes
2	Individual Model	'What do you want our team culture to be in the future?' (5-minute build)	30 minutes

Block	Activity	Question	Time
3	Shared Model	'Combine your models into one Shared Model showing what you want team culture to be.'	30 minutes
	Break		10 minutes
4	Individual Model	• 'Build a key enabler that can help the team.' (2-minute build) • 'Build a key barrier that can slow the team down.' (2-minute build)	30 minutes
5	Landscape Model	'Place your models in the Landscape around the Shared Model.'	30 minutes
6	Final activity	ORID	30 minutes
	Total time		**3 hours**

PATTERN 4

This type of session weaves LSP activities in with 'normal' meeting or workshop content. For example, you might have a day-long conference on leadership. Start the day with some LSP, doing the normal intro and Skills Building and then an Individual Model build. Have those models off to the side as you go through all the other non-LSP content during the day. Then as a wrap-up to the day, do another Individual Model asking for reflections from the entire session.

Block	Activity	Question	Time
1	Intro and Skills Building	'Build a tower with you in it.'	30 minutes
2	Individual Model	'What are the key aspects of good leadership?' (5-minute build)	30 minutes
3	Non-LSP content		6 hours
4	Individual Model	'Reflect on the session. What were your key insights? How has your view of leadership changed?' (5-minute build)	30 minutes
	Total time		**7.5 hours**

Remember, these four patterns are just examples. You can mix and match the activities any way you want.

- Stop after Individual Models
- Do Connections between Individual Models
- Run some scenarios with a Shared Model
- Do a Landscape first, then a Shared Model

- Do a Landscape and then rearrange it in a different Landscape to show new insights

Think of the activities like the LEGO bricks themselves. Combine them anyway you want to achieve the outcome you need.

It's important to note that sessions don't always run to the planned outline. Sometimes activities take more or less time. Always adjust to what the group needs. Slavishly sticking to the plan is bad facilitating. Adapting your plans on the fly is good facilitating.

> Go with the flow. Be prepared to adapt your plans in order to facilitate the learning that is happening in the now rather than the stuff you had planned.
>
> —Ben

12.5 REFINE YOUR QUESTIONS

Once you have your draft session outline, it's time to go back and refine your questions.

The questions you choose to ask in your LSP sessions are the biggest determinant of the success or failure of a session. Ask the wrong question and you won't achieve your objective. Ask the right question and the session is magic.

That leads us to the question: 'What makes a good LSP question?' Here are some principles that help me to craft good questions:

- Low threshold, high ceiling (LTHC) questions
- Single focus, multi-part questions
- Positive/negative questions
- Past/present/future questions
- What and how questions
- Personal perspective questions

12.5.1 LOW THRESHOLD, HIGH CEILING (LTHC) QUESTIONS

The best LSP questions are low threshold, high ceiling.

A low threshold means a question where everyone has an answer. A great example is 'What is a strength you bring to the team?' Every person has a strength and will be able to answer this question.

A high ceiling means a question with a wide range of possible answers. Again, a great example is 'What is a strength you bring to the team?' There are lots of different strengths people could have and so you will get a wide range of answers.

Some good examples:

- 'What's the vision for our team?' Individuals on the team would all have an answer and there's a wide range of possible answers.
- 'How can we improve the customer experience with our service or product?' A group of service designers would all have an answer, and there's a wide range of possible answers.

A bad example is:

- 'What are the third-quarter sales results at our company?' If you don't have that specific information, you can't answer it (high threshold). Also, there is only one right answer (low ceiling).

There are two reasons why LTHC questions are so important in LEGO Serious Play:

- **Low threshold** drives 100 percent engagement. Everyone has to have an answer so everyone can build.
- **High ceiling** drives exposure to a wide range of diverse ideas. This helps us change our thinking, see connections and arrive at new insights.

12.5.2 SINGLE FOCUS, MULTI-PART QUESTIONS

It's important to craft a question that has a single focus.

Never ask double-barrelled questions like 'What are the risks and benefits of this project?' People get mentally overloaded and don't know what to build.

One question, one focus.

If you want to ask more questions, do it as a multi-part question.

For example, 'What are the benefits of this project?' Let participants build for four minutes. Before they share, ask them to build again. 'Now add into your model some risks for the project.' This allows them to focus on building one thing at a time. They then can share both aspects of their model or story at the same time.

Multi-part questions are great when you want to dive deeper.

I could ask: 'What is the core identity of our company?' or convert that into a multi-part question:

1. 'What is the internal identity of our company?' Build (five minutes), put to the side.
2. 'What is the external identity of our company?' Build (five minutes), put to the side.
3. 'What is the aspirational identity of our company?' Build (five minutes), then share all three.

Another example is:

1. 'What strengths do you bring to the team?' Build (five minutes).
2. 'Now add in your x-factor. Something that no one else knows about.' Build (two minutes).

That last example shows another interesting variation. Get people to build the model and then do a small addition to it. This style of question keeps people on a single focus but adds depth to the build and story.

Overall, doing a multi-part question can add layers, angles and depth to a build and the resulting conversation.

12.5.3 POSITIVE VERSUS NEGATIVE QUESTIONS

You can ask either positive or negative questions in an LSP session.

By negative questions, I mean 'What's a challenge you're facing?' or 'What's the biggest barrier?'

Those questions are great for uncovering elements you need to work through.

Over time, though, I'm asking more positive questions. Studies have shown that you're more creative when you're positive, happy and future-focused. Positive questions also make for a more enjoyable session.

That's not to say that you should shy away from the negative questions. If you need to, go there. But know what space that's putting you and your participants in.

There's a field of organisational development called appreciative inquiry. It focuses on what gives life to a system. Where are the successes? Let's learn from those and build on them. It's a strength-based approach.

Appreciative inquiry as a practice acknowledges that problems exist in organisations, but it chooses to focus on visions of a successful future to help drive change. People who run appreciative inquiry workshops have a wonderful phrase: 'Words create worlds'. What you talk about and the questions you ask create the world where the conversation lives. Starting with 'challenges' and 'barriers' sets a tone for the session. Starting with 'successes' and 'possibilities' sets a different tone.

Most of my LSP sessions now use positive appreciative inquiry questions.

12.5.4 PAST/PRESENT/FUTURE QUESTIONS

Another lens I use to craft my questions is thinking about which part of time I want to focus on.

You could ask questions about:

- **Past experiences** to reflect and gather lessons learned

- **Current state** to make sense of what is happening now
- **Possible futures** to plan where you want to go

Your LSP questions and sessions can tap into any of these timeframes.

- I've run sessions where we have built:
- The current state and then a path to the future state
- Past experiences to inform a future vision (as is done in appreciative inquiry)

The vision of a future state and then worked backwards, outlining the steps on how to get there

Any of these combinations work.

12.5.5 WHAT AND HOW QUESTIONS

Questions that start with 'What' and 'How' work best for LSP.

'Who', 'Where' and 'When' questions are often too specific and don't work well.

'Why' questions can work, but you must be cautious with them. Sometimes asking *why* can feel too confrontational. Why questions often require people to provide reasons and justifications behind something. This can make people defensive and it can potentially break the psychological safety of sessions. These questions can be powerful, but be very cautious with them. Pick your group and topic wisely. Are they a mature team with open communication and trust in each other? *Why* questions could be good. Are they a new team establishing themselves? Stick to *what* and *how* questions.

Overall, I've found *what* and *how* questions the best.[7]

12.5.6 PERSONAL PERSPECTIVE QUESTIONS

Personal perspective questions are great LSP questions. Asking someone to build things about their own experiences, their own skills or their own views always results in powerful stories and great discussions.

- 'Think of a time when you were the most creative in your life. What was the situation and what drove that creativity?'
- 'What is your leadership style?'
- 'What does [insert any topic] mean to you?'
- 'Reflecting on the project, what lessons did you learn?'

7 If you're interested in diving deeper into the wording of questions, check out the 'Question Ladder' by an organisation called NESTA: https://diytoolkit.org/tools/question-ladder/.

The question doesn't always have to be about someone's own perspective. Shifting focus and taking a customer's view or a colleague's view works too. But tapping into a personal perspective is really powerful.

12.5.7 THE BEST LSP QUESTION

If I had to describe the best LSP question, it would be:

- Low threshold, high ceiling
- Single focus, multi-part
- Positive
- What...? or How...?
- Tapping into a personal perspective

Other types of questions can work, too, but I've found these types of questions always lead to great conversations and great outcomes.

12.5.8 HOW TO USE THESE PRINCIPLES

Take the broad questions that you found at the start of the design process and see how they match up with some of these principles.

The two key things to ask yourself are:

- Is my question low threshold, high ceiling? If not, how can I change the question to ensure

100 percent engagement and a diverse set of answers?
- Does my question have a single focus? If not, how can I split it up into a multi-part question?

Make sure that you get both of those aspects right. But the rest of the principles are about making choices:

- Am I asking a positive or negative question? Both are fine; just know what choice you're making.
- Which timeframe am I focusing on: the past, the present or the future?
- Am I starting the question with 'What' or 'How'? Or do I have a group that could handle a 'Why' question?
- Which perspective am I asking the builder to take: their own or someone else's?

As you refine your questions, look back at the outline you've created. Sometimes, as you change the questions, you'll need to change the flow or choice of activities too.

Overall, the skill of crafting the right question is a skill that goes beyond LEGO Serious Play. It's a key skill in whatever work you do. The right question opens up powerful conversations and insights. The wrong question leads to wasted time and missed opportunities.

As you get more experience running LSP sessions, you'll get a good feel for the wording of your questions and the answers they lead to.

> Spend more time than you think getting the right question right and considering it from different angles.
>
> —Guy

12.6 WHERE TO USE THE POWER OF LSP

One last thing to consider with this whole session design process is where you want to use the power of LSP.

You could use LSP:

- At the start of a longer session to open up conversation and explore ideas.
- At the end of a longer session to reflect on what was learnt or to crystallise insights.
- At a high level, asking questions like 'What is leadership?' 'What is innovation?' or 'What challenges is this project facing?'
- To dive deeper after generating those types of high-level insights with other non-LSP techniques. An

example would be to get the group to generate the challenges a project is facing, using Post-it notes, and then flip to LSP mode to generate solutions.

Now that you know the LSP method and how to design sessions, the key choice is where to apply it. Should you use LSP at the start, the middle or the end of a session? At a high level or for diving deeper? For the whole session or only part of it, weaving in other techniques? There's no one right answer. But as you start to think of your first sessions, think about where best to apply the power of LSP.

12.7 CONCLUSION

Let's recap how to design an LSP session:

- Decide whether LSP is the right tool
- Find your key questions
- Draft the session outline
- Refine the questions

In this chapter, you saw a couple of examples of different session outlines. In the next chapter, we'll go through even more examples.

Chapter 13

EXAMPLE SESSIONS

A great way to improve your sessions is to look at examples. Get inspired and pick out the key elements that you want to include in your own sessions. But remember that every session you run should be customised to your topic and your audience.

The examples below are listed by length of time. There is a one-hour session, a range of two-hour sessions and some longer three-hour-plus sessions. Each topic on the list below is a separate session.

For each session outline, I've assumed it's a first-time group and I have included the full thirty-minute intro and Skills Building component. As always, if the group know LSP already, do one of the shorter activities mentioned at the end of chapter 6.

ONE-HOUR SESSION

Lunch and Learn (I'll explain what this means below. It's not about providing lunch!)

TWO-HOUR SESSIONS

- Team vision
- Collaboration
- Project kick-off
- Retrospectives
- Ideation
- Coaching
- Innovation: barriers and solutions
- Business Model Canvas
- Recruitment

THREE-HOUR-PLUS SESSIONS

- Team Identity
- Team Strategy

13.1 ONE-HOUR SESSION: LUNCH AND LEARN

This is the first session that I would encourage you to run. It's a simple way to introduce LSP to a group of people and is easy for you to facilitate. Do this with friends, family or as an introduction to LSP at work.

Just an aside, it's called a Lunch and Learn because it's traditionally done over lunchtime. This is a way for people to experience LSP without taking away from 'work time'. It is a fun way to spend your lunch hour. You don't have to provide food for people. Encourage them to bring their own food along or eat beforehand or afterwards. Or don't even do it over lunchtime; find a time that suits your audience. The key here is that it's a short, one-hour taster session.

Objective: Introduce People to the LEGO Serious Play Method

Block	Activity	Question	Time
1	Intro and Skills Building	'Build a tower with you in it.'	25 minutes
2	Individual Model	'What is something important that your company (or industry) is not talking enough about?' (5-minute build)	25 minutes
3	Final activity	Q&A + What else LSP can be used for	10 minutes
	Total time		**1 hour**

The Individual Model question can be almost anything. In the past, I've asked questions like:

- 'What value do you bring to your clients? Add in how that makes them feel.'
- 'What is your vision for the team in the next two years?'
- 'What are you excited about for 2020?'

You'll also notice that for blocks 1 and 2, I've shaved five minutes off the usual time of thirty minutes. I wouldn't normally do that, but for a Lunch and Learn it's okay to do those builds a little more quickly. For normal sessions that have important objectives, don't cut time anywhere; you'll need it all!

13.2 TWO-HOUR SESSIONS

For your second session, I would recommend running a two-hour session like the ones below. The session might not be on one of these exact topics, but using this style of session is a great way to build up your LSP facilitation skills.

TEAM VISION

Objective: Create a Shared Understanding of the Team's Future Vision and the Actions to Achieve It

Block	Activity	Question	Time
1	Intro and Skills Building	'Build a tower with you in it.'	30 minutes
2	Individual Model	'What is your vision for the team in the next two years?' (5-minute build)	30 minutes
3	Shared Model	'Combine your models into one Shared Model showing what you want the team vision to be.'	30 minutes
4	Final activity	ORID	30 minutes
	Total time		**2 hours**

COLLABORATION

Objective: Enhance Collaboration Within the Team and Between Teams

Block	Activity	Question	Time
1	Intro and Skills Building	'Build a tower with you in it.'	30 minutes

Block	Activity	Question	Time
2	Individual Model	'How can we work more collaboratively within the team?' After the initial build, add in 'How can we work more collaboratively with other teams?' (5- + 2-minute build)	30 minutes
3	Shared Model	'Combine your models into one Shared Model showing how we can collaborate better'.	30 minutes
4	Final activity	ORID	30 minutes
	Total time		**2 hours**

PROJECT KICK-OFF

Objective: Get a Shared Understanding of What Will Drive Project Success

Block	Activity	Question	Time
1	Intro and Skills Building	'Build a tower with you in it.'	30 minutes
2	Individual Model	'What are the factors that will drive success in this project?' After the initial build, add in 'What is your role in that?' (4- + 2-minute build)	30 minutes

Block	Activity	Question	Time
3	Shared Model	'Combine your models into one Shared Model showing project success.'	30 minutes
4	Final activity	ORID	30 minutes
	Total time		**2 hours**

RETROSPECTIVES

Objective: Highlight Lessons Learned and Areas for Future Improvement

Block	Activity	Question	Time
1	Intro and Skills Building	'Build a tower with you in it.'	30 minutes
2	Individual Model	'What went well?' (3-minute build) 'What needs improvement?' (3-minute build)	30 minutes
3	Landscape Model	'Put your models into the centre of the table and place them in relation to each other to form a landscape of themes.'	30 minutes
4	Final activity	ORID	30 minutes
	Total time		**2 hours**

IDEATION

Objective: Generate Ideas on any Topic

Block	Activity	Question	Time
1	Intro and Skills Building	'Build a tower with you in it.'	30 minutes
2	Individual Model	'How could we [for example] open up new business opportunities for our division?' (3-minute build x 2.)	30 minutes
3	Landscape Model	'Put your models into the centre of the table and place them in relation to each other to form a landscape of ideas.'	30 minutes
4	Final activity	ORID	30 minutes
	Total time		**2 hours**

INNOVATION: BARRIERS AND SOLUTIONS

Objective: Surface the Factors Stopping the Company from Being More Innovative

Block	Activity	Question	Time
1	Intro and Skills Building	'Build a tower with you in it.'	30 minutes

Block	Activity	Question	Time
2	Individual Model	'What is stopping us from being more innovative? Go beyond the obvious answers of time and money.' (3- minute build x 2)	30 minutes
3	Landscape Model	'Put your models into the centre of the table and place them in relation to each other to form a landscape of barriers.'	30 minutes
4	Final activity	ORID	30 minutes
	Total time		**2 hours**

or

Objective: Discover Novel Ways to Overcome Innovation Barriers

Use Post-it notes to come up with the barriers or challenges to innovation. Select certain barriers to work on. Then flip to LSP mode.

Block	Activity	Question	Time
1	Intro and Skills Building	'Build a tower with you in it.'	30 minutes

Block	Activity	Question	Time
2	Individual Model	'What is a solution to overcome that barrier/ challenge?' (3-minute build x 3)	30 minutes
3	Landscape Model	'Put your models into the centre of the table and place them in relation to each other to form a landscape of solutions.'	30 minutes
4	Final activity	ORID	30 minutes
	Total time		**2 hours**

BUSINESS MODEL CANVAS

Objective: Use LSP to Help Fill Out the Business Model Canvas

The Business Model Canvas is a visual tool developed by a company called Strategyzer. It's used to analyse business models, value propositions, customer segments and many more aspects of a business. If you're interested in knowing more about it, just google 'Business Model Canvas'.

You may never use it, but it's a great example of how to combine LSP with other visual tools. The key to combining LSP with the Business Model Canvas is to only use the LSP method where it adds value. Sections such as

Value Proposition, Customer Segments and Customer Relationships all work well with LSP. For the other sections, it's better to go back to the normal way the tool is filled in, with Post-it notes.

This highlights an important point when combining LSP with other methods: only use LSP where it adds value through its story and metaphorical approach.

Block	Activity	Question	Time
1	Intro and Skills Building	'Build a tower with you in it.'	30 minutes
2	Individual Model	'What is our value proposition? What value do we deliver to the customer?' (5-minute build)	30 minutes
3	Shared Model	'Combine your models into one Shared Model showing our value proposition.'	30 minutes
4	Final activity	ORID	30 minutes
	Total time		**2 hours**

If you have more time, you can extend this session to include another section. After the Shared Model, include this before going to the final activity:

Block	Activity	Question	Time
3a	Individual Model	'Who are our key customers? Include what our relationship is with them.' (3-minute build x 3)	30 minutes
3b	Landscape Model	'Place your models around the Shared Model, showing how different customer segments relate to the value proposition.'	30 minutes

RECRUITMENT

Objective: Get to Know the Real Person Behind the Interview

Block	Activity	Question	Time
1	Intro and Skills Building	'Build a tower with you in it.'	10 minutes
2	Individual Model	Any behavioural interview question you're already asking. An example: 'Think of a time when you have been part of a successful team. What factors drove that success? What was your role in that?' (5-minute build)	10 minutes

Block	Activity	Question	Time
3	Individual Model	Another behavioural interview question	10 minutes
	Total time		**30–60 minutes**

You'll notice for this session and the following one, the blocks of time are only ten minutes. Using LSP one-on-one speeds up the whole process because you don't have five to six people sharing their model or story.

COACHING

Objective: Help an Individual Tackle a Problem Using the GROW Coaching Model and LSP

Block	Activity	Question	Time
1	Intro and Skills Building	'Build a tower with you in it.'	10 minutes
2	Individual Model	Goal: 'What is your goal?' (5-minute build)	10 minutes
3	Individual Model	Reality: 'What is the reality of the situation?' (5-minute build)	10 minutes
4	Individual Model	Option: 'What could you do? What else?' (2-minute build x 3)	10 minutes

Block	Activity	Question	Time
5	Individual Model	Will: 'What will you do? What is the first step?' (5-minute build)	10 minutes
	Total time		**50 minutes**

For this example (and, really, any others where you are combining LSP with another method), remember to only use LSP where it adds value. If you prefer, do some parts of the process with LSP and some with your normal approach. For the GROW model, I would revert to normal conversation with pen and paper for the last section, Will.

13.3 THREE-HOUR-PLUS SESSIONS

My recommendation is that if you want to run the longer three-hour-plus sessions below, you should seek further advice beyond this book. This is not because there's anything super special about them—there are no 'tricks' that you're missing out on—it's simply that as the session goes longer, you start to get more complicated designs with more themes running through them and the stakes get higher. We're talking about team identity and strategy work: topics that you only have one shot to get right.

As you look through the outlines below, you'll recognise all the activities; they're the same ones you have learnt in this book. But the facilitation skills a person needs to run these sessions goes up another level. You need to ensure that you get everything you need out of each activity and that it builds to the outcome you're seeking.

If you feel you've got the facilitation mastery to do that, then go for it! But my recommendation is to at least chat with a more experienced LSP facilitator and get some advice on your situation.

TEAM IDENTITY

Objective: Create a Shared Understanding of the Team's Future Identity and Each Individual's Role in That

This Session is great for a new team finding their feet.

Block	Activity	Question	Time
1	Intro and Skills Building	'Build a tower with you in it.'	30 minutes
2	Individual Model (This build is focused on the individual person.)	• 'Who are you on the team right now? Build your strengths and your identity.' (5-minute build) • 'Now add in a hidden talent, something no one knows about.' (2-minute build) • Share and put the model to the side.	30 minutes

Block	Activity	Question	Time
3	Individual Model (This build is focused on the team.)	'What do you want team life to be in the future?' (5-minute build)	30 minutes
	Break		15 minutes
4	Shared Model	'Combine your models into one Shared Model of what you want team life to be.'	30 minutes
5	Landscape Model	• Bring back the individual identity models that were set aside earlier. • 'Place your identity model in the landscape around the team life model showing where you feel most connected to and why.'	15 minutes
6	Connections	'Place a connection between your model and the central model highlighting where you can contribute most.'	15 minutes
7	Final activity	ORID + Kanban board	30 minutes
	Total time		**3.5 hours**

TEAM STRATEGY

Objective: Create a Shared Understanding of the Team's Identity and the Broader External Ecosystem

The fundamental difference between this team strategy session and the team identity session above is:

The team identity session above looks at individuals on the team and then what the team identity is. Its focus is on the team's internal workings. This session works best when the team is new, has gone through a lot of change or is unsure of who they are as a team.

The team strategy session below starts with who the team are (and want to be) and then focuses externally on who is impacting the team. It works best when the team is more established, knows their roles and is confident with who they are. They can then focus on dealing with the external factors to drive high performance.[8]

Block	Activity	Question	Time
1	Intro and Skills Building	'Build a tower with you in it.'	30 minutes

8 Both the team identity and team strategy session outlines were inspired by the first two (and only) session outlines that the LEGO Group developed in the early 2000s.

Block	Activity	Question	Time
2	Individual Model	• 'Who are we at our core right now? Build our internal team identity.' (5-minute build) • Keep models.	30 minutes
3	Individual Model	• 'What is our current external team identity? That is how we are viewed by the rest of the business.' (5-minute build) • Keep models.	30 minutes
4	Individual Model	• 'Who do we want to be in the future? Build our aspirational team identity.' (5-minute build) • Keep models.	30 minutes
	Break		15 minutes
5	Shared Model	'Combine your internal, external and aspirational identity models into one Shared Model of who we are and who we want to be.'	30 minutes

Block	Activity	Question	Time
6	Individual Model (Agents)	• 'Who or what are the Agents influencing us right now?' (2-minute build) • 'Who or what are the Agents that could have the biggest influence on us in the future?' (2-minute build) • Depending on numbers of participants and how big a table you have, you could do multiple rounds of each of these questions.	30 minutes
7	Landscape Model	• 'Place your Agent models in the landscape around the central team identity model showing where you feel they are related'. • For this Agent activity, you can let participants either build all the Agents and then place them or interweave the two activities and build one round of Agents and then place them, then build another round of Agents and place them, etc.	30 minutes
	Lunch		1 hour

Block	Activity	Question	Time
8	Connections	• 'Place a connection between an Agent and the Shared Model.' • 'Place a connection between two Agent models.'	30 minutes
9	Scenarios	Play out three scenarios to see how the team respond in real time to a changing environment.	60 minutes
10	Final activity	ORID + Kanban board	30 minutes
	Total time		**7 hours**

Depending on time and your objective, you could stop after the Shared Model or after the Agents. You could leave out the Connections or run the scenarios earlier. There are so many options!

While this session was pitched at the team strategy level, you could run it at the department level, company level or industry level. The same activities above are useful no matter what level you are looking at.

13.4 CONCLUSION

In this chapter, you've seen twelve different session outlines ranging from one hour to seven-plus hours.

Remember: they are just examples to learn from and pick apart. I always recommend you custom design each session. And while many of them have followed those common patterns, you can mix and match the LSP activities in anyway you want (even with other non-LSP activities!).

Chapter 14

THE SCIENCE OF LEGO SERIOUS PLAY

Now that you know the mechanics of a session, it's interesting to find out why this method works. It may look like people are just playing with bricks, but there is some amazing science going on just below the surface in an LSP session.

Why do you need to know about the science of LSP? Sometimes people ask, and it's good to show how solid the foundation is. It's also good to know what levers you, as a facilitator, are pulling when you use LSP. By understanding the why, you can adjust your style to get even better results.

There are a range of foundational scientific theories that underpin LSP:

- Constructivism and constructionism
- Flow
- Hand-brain connection
- Play
- Metaphor
- Storytelling

Below is a short summary of each of these areas. Think of them as a jumping-off point for further research, if you're interested.

14.1 CONSTRUCTIVISM AND CONSTRUCTIONISM

Constructivism is a theory of how we acquire new knowledge. It says we 'construct' new knowledge based on the combination of our existing mental models and the new experiences coming in.

The key feature is that we are active knowledge-builders rather than passive receivers of information.

Constructionism takes this idea of us as active knowledge builders a step further. The theory says that the best way to build new knowledge is when we create a physical object in the world: something that we can see, use, share and investigate.

If we create something in the world, we set up this wonderful loop:

- We have knowledge in our mind.
- We create a physical object about it in the world (it could be a drawing, a prototype, or in our case, an LSP model).
- By that act of creation, we see that topic differently.
- We interact with the object. Others interact with the object. That interaction makes us see the object and topic differently.
- Creating and interacting with this physical object changes our mental model.
- Which leads us to construct something different and the loop begins again.

New knowledge, new connections and new insights are the primary aim of LSP. Constructivism and constructionism are the knowledge and learning theories that underpin that.

14.2 FLOW

We've all experienced being in flow. It's when you're so in the moment in an activity that you lose yourself and all sense of time. You see it in professional athletes who are 'in the zone' or in yourself when you get lost in a hobby or reading a book.

So why is flow useful? It's a state of peak experience (and sometimes peak performance). That's what we're looking for in LSP. People get out of their own way, get into flow and have a different experience leading to a different result.

I've had many comments like 'Wow, we've been doing this for three hours! Time has flown.' That's not just because LSP is fun. The rhythm of an LSP session is specifically designed to encourage flow in the participants.

There's nothing you need to do specifically as a facilitator to encourage flow. Follow the steps and flow will happen.

14.3 HAND-BRAIN CONNECTION

One of the key things that makes us special as humans is our hands, and we don't use them as much as we could in this modern digital world.

Research has shown that people who use their hands are better problem solvers.

You can find images online of the 'sensory motor cortical homunculus'. The grotesque figure in the images is a representation of how much of the surface of our brain is devoted to different parts of the body. The bigger the part on the figure, the more surface of the brain is devoted to that part of the body. Go Google it and check it out; it's really bizarre.

What is the biggest part on this grotesque figure? The hands. The hands are by far the most brain-connected part of our anatomy. They help us access our knowledge in a different way. One LSP facilitator brilliantly describes our hands as 'another search engine for the brain'.

Our hands can help us to think. In LSP we call it hand-thinking and hand-knowledge.

In this modern world, we've forgotten this ability. Rediscovering it through LSP is an amazing way to tap into what you already know, in a different way.

I've had many people surprised at what they built. It was inside them all along; they just weren't accessing it properly.

The use of the hands as a way of thinking is one of the unique features of LSP.

14.4 PLAY

We all know the benefits of play when we see it in children. They get to test out new skills and try new ways of interacting and experiencing the world. Those are attributes we want to bring into the world of work too. But

I want to go past the obvious and focus on three areas where play might surprise you:

- The artificial separation of work and play
- What play at work looks like
- Why playfulness is the thing

Somewhere in history, work and play got separated (my suspicion is it was the industrial revolution's fault). Play is something that children do to learn, but adults don't bring play to work! Play is seen as the opposite of work. Work during the day, play at night and on weekends. Never the two should meet.

That worked over the last hundred years when you wanted efficiency in your workplace. But efficiency only gets you so far. You don't 'efficient' your way to new products and services or new ways of doing things. Work needs a helping hand, and play can help.

Play at work has an awkward history. It's been very conservative. 'Let's do something fun, like a team-building event' or 'Let's include pool tables or arcade games in the break room'. Employees can go off, play and then come back refreshed, hopefully with some benefits being transferred back to their work like greater health or well-being. That's fine and a laudable goal, but it's underselling the power of play to change the way we work.

Play shouldn't be something we do over there. It should be a way we do work right here.

A better approach is to look at playfulness rather than play: a mindset rather than an activity.

We can co-opt play and its many benefits to achieve a work purpose. Think of play and playfulness as a mode of thinking, a mode of being we can slip into when we need it and when it can help us to achieve our aims.

That's why I love LSP. It's not 'Let's go over there and play and then come back to work'. It's 'Let's look at this business challenge in a playful way. Maybe a playful lens will give us the insights we need to make a breakthrough.'

Like the hand, play is a tool we've forgotten about. LSP helps us tap into those skills that we all innately possess.

One of the great things about using LEGO is that playfulness is built right into it. People see LEGO and they naturally fall into play mode.

14.5 METAPHOR

Metaphors are all around us. In 1980, George Lakoff and Mark Johnson wrote the book *Metaphors We Live By*. They lifted the lid on how metaphors are the foundation to our language and our thinking.

A metaphor is the use of one thing to represent something else, for the purpose of comparison or symbolism. We relate the two things, transferring some (but not all) characteristics from one to the other to help us understand.

Metaphors abound. Email anyone? It's really just a bunch of ones and zeroes, but we liken it to sending a real letter.

Lakoff and Johnson use the example of argument. The underlying metaphor of argument is war. We defend our ideas and attack our opponents.

But why can't the underlying metaphor be dance? Argument is a dance where we engage and interact with our arguing partners to come to a wonderful performance and outcome.

Almost everything has an underlying metaphor that shapes our language and our actions. If you really think about it, we can only ever 'know' something new by relating it to something we already know.

What is light? Is it a wave or a particle? It has some characteristics of both, but it's neither. It's something we don't have a solid metaphor for and so our understanding of light is lacking.

Take the topic of taxation. People speak of tax 'relief'. The underlying metaphor is that taxation is a burden or an illness that we need saving from. What if the underlying metaphor of taxation was investment instead of illness. Paying tax is an investment in society, and we receive the dividends of society, a health system, education, infrastructure and so on. That would change the conversation around taxation.

Politicians are very good at anchoring their desires to a metaphor to change the public debate. Global warming, climate change, climate emergency, climate crisis. Whatever your politics are, it's interesting to think of the subtle differences in the underlying metaphors for each of those phrases. Take any public topic and think of the underlying metaphor. Just knowing what metaphor is driving the conversation helps you to better understand what is happening.

So how does this relate to LSP? It's a metaphorical tool. From the very start of a session, we encourage people to build using metaphors. We do this because when you make comparisons through metaphor, new insights can emerge.

On another level, using metaphor in LSP can help us supplant existing metaphors with new ones.

I have this little saying: 'Change the metaphor, change the behaviour'.

Changing the underlying metaphor through which people view an issue may open up new paths for action. LSP as a tool can be used to change deep-seated metaphors, leading to more sustainable behavioural change.

14.6 STORYTELLING

While we live in an era of big data, people are realising that stories are what really stick.

That's because our brains are literally wired for story. Stories are virtual reality simulations that allow us to experience events without needing to be there.

When you listen to someone tell a riveting story, your heart rate changes, your brain chemistry changes, and you are there experiencing that event and learning all you need to without placing yourself in danger.

Story connects, story motivates, story sticks.

LEGO Serious Play, at its heart, is a storytelling technique. Every model built has a story told about it. The ability to tell a story is in all of us. I see it time and again in LSP sessions. Even when I don't instruct groups to form a story for a group build, they do it anyway. It's innate.

Story is another one of these skills that we've forgotten about in the modern business world. LSP allows us to tap into our storytelling abilities and be enthralled by the stories of others.

14.7 THE SCIENCE OF LSP

Knowledge theories, like constructivism and constructionism, getting in flow, using the hand-brain connection, co-opting play, uncovering metaphor and blowing our minds with storytelling all come together under the surface to make LSP the powerful method it is. If you are keen to dive even deeper into the science, head to *www.lspmethod.com/science*. You'll find a wonderful document put together by the LEGO Group in the early days of LSP.

Chapter 15

RANDOM PILE

When I was young, I would build LEGO models, and at the end, there were always a few random pieces left.

This chapter is those leftover pieces. These are the super important topics that didn't quite fit in anywhere else.

15.1 THE BARRIERS TO LSP

Now that you know the LSP method, the only thing stopping you is getting people in the room to do it. Once they're in the session, LSP works its magic. But there are barriers you need to overcome before that.

People have a lot of preconceptions about LEGO, from it being a child's toy to its use in 'fun' team-building activities. The biggest challenge you will face is not learning the method or getting the method to work;

those are easy. The biggest challenge is shifting people's thinking to look at LSP as a serious business tool that can get serious results.

I need to overcome these barriers from an external consultant perspective, but this same approach works if you need to convince someone within your organisation to do a session.

It's all in how you talk about LSP. In a moment, I'll show you what I do when I sit down with someone and talk LSP with them. But the biggest tip I have for you is this: bring some LEGO along and get them to experience the LSP method.

It may seem obvious, but for a long time, I didn't do it. I just talked about it to people. But by bringing LEGO along, you can show them, rather than tell them. Once they get their hands on the bricks, most people get it straight away.

However, I don't start with that. Here's what I do when I sit down to explain LSP: I go through some of the same material from the workshop introduction that I explained in chapter 5. The people you are talking to have the same questions as the participants in your workshops.

WHAT IS LSP?

I start with 'LEGO Serious Play was developed by the LEGO Group in the late 1990s and early 2000s as a better way to do corporate strategy. It's now moved beyond the

LEGO Group and beyond strategy. It's used as a meeting and workshop method to get people highly engaged and thinking differently.

'In a session, you ask people questions and they answer them by building LEGO models. They're not building literal things but rather using metaphor and storytelling, and from that, they get new insights about their work.'

WHO USES IT AND FOR WHAT?

'I've used it with the likes of Google, KPMG, Ernst & Young and [include an organisation in your industry that uses LSP. There will be one].

'They use it for innovation, strategy, customer experience and [insert the use you want to use LSP for].'

WHY DOES IT WORK?

'It works because it engages all the talent in the room. It's creative, it's collaborative and there's a lot of good science that underpins it.'

If you feel the person needs to hear it, go into the science. I like to focus on the use of our hands and how powerful that is in problem solving.

MECHANICS OF A SESSION

At this point people usually say to me, 'But what do you do in a session?'

I explain the four steps: 'We decide on a topic beforehand and develop some questions. Then in Step 1 of the workshop, I ask the question. In Step 2, people build their answer to that question in LEGO, individually at first and then later on in groups. In Step 3, they share the story of their model, their answer to the question, with those on their table. Once everyone has done that we reflect on it and capture the insights in Step 4. Then we do it again with a different question.'

OUTCOMES

People then ask, 'What are the outcomes?'

I say, 'It's very flexible, so we can mould the outcomes to what you are after. Usually, the outcomes are a set of actions that people can do back at work. This can be individual actions or team actions in the form of a Kanban board. You also get wonderful photos and videos of the session as a record of the conversation and insights.'

WILL IT WORK?

People then ask, 'How do people respond? I don't think my people will like it.'

I say, 'There is a set way that I do the warm-up, and it never fails to get people into the method. I did a workshop for the car company Lexus when they were going through a huge transformation. I had big burly car guys coming into the workshop with their arms crossed, saying 'Why am I here? I've got real work to do.' By the end of the session, they were the ones wanting more. Because they realised it's not about the LEGO; it's about having a better conversation, and they wanted more of it.'

ACTIVITY

At this point I usually ask the person if they want to do a little activity to see how it works.

I then take them through the 'build a tower with you in it' activity from the Skills Building. I give some examples of the use of metaphor and then do the tower activity with them.

NEXT STEPS

The last part of the conversation is about what a full session would look like. If they are keen at this point, I explore their objectives and talk about doing a two- or three-and-a-half-hour session.

If they are still unsure, I've found one last idea that can help some people get over their barriers to LSP. I talk about doing either a one-hour Lunch and Learn (which we covered in chapter 13) or I use the phrase 'pilot session' or 'test session'.

Both of these options reduce the perceived risk of doing an LSP session. A one-hour session over lunch or just running a 'pilot' is a lot easier for some people to commit to than a two- or three-and-a-half-hour session that takes up 'work time'. Obviously, you can't get much done in those short sessions, but as LSP works its magic, this might be the start of a series of sessions.

This whole process I've described, with questions and activities, takes around thirty minutes. It is extremely successful in getting people to do LSP. But in the end, if someone doesn't really want to do it, don't force it. If they're not on board now, the LSP session won't go well anyway.

15.2 THE BIGGEST MISTAKE YOU'LL MAKE WITH LSP

The LSP method works really well. It's one of the most consistent facilitation techniques I've ever used. But there is one big mistake that trips up every new LSP facilitator: trying to do too much in too short a timeframe.

I fell into this trap when I first started. I learnt all these shiny new activities and I would try to cram them all into a session. Or I would think I could achieve this massive objective in just a short two-hour session.

What I learnt was that it is better to do fewer activities and let them breathe. Ask fewer questions and leave more time for conversation and sparking of insights. That's why I stick to the thirty-minute-block design principle. It forces me to leave the proper time for the activities. You could leave even more time for each activity if you wanted.

New facilitators often jump at any opportunity to do LSP and say yes to the one-hour session during which the client wants to achieve world peace. The success of your LSP sessions are in large part due to choosing the right objective and the minimum number of activities to achieve that.

Here is a timeframe guide I use:

- **One Hour**. Get to experience the basic LSP method. You can't achieve any real objective.
- **Two Hours**. Super focused objective on one topic.
- **Three and a Half Hours or More**. Unpack a multilayered topic from different angles.

Of course, all this depends on the numbers of participants and whether the group already know LSP. But always keep in mind that less is more. Don't fall into the same trap that I did and try to do too much in one session. If it's a big topic, explore it over multiple sessions.

15.3 TRADEMARK GUIDELINES

There is a set of trademark guidelines that the LEGO Group puts out for LEGO Serious Play.

The guidelines are updated every few years, so check for the latest.[9] But here is my take on the most recent one from 2017.

The overriding message is that you never want to give the impression that the LEGO Group endorses what you do.

The guidelines are available online, but here are three important aspects:

- **Trademarks and Logos**. Don't ever use the LEGO logo. The word LEGO and the phrase Serious Play are both registered trademarks of the LEGO Group. You can use them, but you need to put a ® symbol after each, like this: LEGO® Serious Play®. You only need to do the ® symbol the first time you use it on a web page or in a document. After that, further references on the page can drop the ®.

9 LEGO Group, 'LEGO SERIOUS PLAY Trademark Guidelines Version 2017,' accessed 12 January 2020, https://www.lego.com/en-us/seriousplay/contact.

- **Workshops Titles.** For workshops that use LSP, you are never running a 'LEGO Serious Play Workshop'. You are running a 'Strategy Workshop using LEGO Serious Play' or an 'Innovation Workshop using the LEGO Serious Play method'. Don't put the LEGO Serious Play bit at the front. You are always '[Doing something] using LEGO Serious Play'.
- **Use of Images.** The guidelines state that you can't use photos that have 'Iconic and/or emphasized use of the LEGO® Minifigures and/or the LEGO bricks/knobs'. They go on to say, 'The photo material can include training sessions with the use of LEGO bricks and elements but without detailed focus on the LEGO products'. What does that mean in practice? Examples are given in the guidelines. The way I approach it, you can use photos from LSP sessions that show models and people building them, just don't get too close to the models! The LEGO Group don't want it to look like LEGO marketing material. Of course, this is just for using photos on websites and documents. You and your participants are quite welcome to take photos of whatever you want, however you want.

There's more to the trademark guidelines, so read the latest version. Also, note that they are guidelines; there are no LEGO police coming to take your bricks away. But it's important to adhere to the guidelines and work with the LEGO Group to keep the LEGO Serious Play brand strong.

15.4 DOING LSP ONLINE

One new frontier I want to introduce you to is doing LSP online. It sounds crazy that you can do a hands-on method in a digital way, but you can. It's still about physically using LEGO bricks and building with your hands, but then using digital technologies like video calls and online platforms to share your models and insights.

You can't use all of the LSP activities, and the experience is not as powerful as being in the same room at the same time, but there are ways to do it.

There are three distinct scenarios in which you could use LSP in a digital way. In all scenarios, people in each location will need their own LEGO.

- **Multiple teams** in different locations. In this instance, you can do all the LSP activities (Individual, Shared, Landscape, Connections) as normal, locally with each team. When it comes

time to share stories from a Shared Model or Landscape Model, you can do that via video call. This situation is akin to running multiple tables in one room.
- **Individual people** in lots of different locations. In this instance, you can do Individual Models easily, sharing via video calls. Landscape Models and Connections are possible with the use of an online tool I mentioned earlier, Padlet. Shared Models aren't possible.
- **Asynchronous** LSP. That is, doing LSP at different times and in different physical locations. An example of this is posting a question to an internal social media platform and telling people that sometime over the next week, they should take five minutes, build their model and post their story (either written or in video format). They should also take the time to read the other stories. For this type of LSP, only Individual Models are possible, but you could come together after a week and run Landscapes and Connections using Padlet.

We're still at the very beginning of understanding what's possible with LSP online, but it's an exciting frontier the community is exploring.

15.5 GOING ROGUE

It's time to confess that I've gone a little rogue and changed small parts of the traditional LSP method. Over the years and through many sessions, I've adapted and evolved the method to make it better. The changes have mostly been at the start of the method: the four steps and the Skills Building. If you're keen to know more details about the changes, turn to appendix 2: Going Rogue. Enjoy!

15.6 FURTHER LEARNING

This book is only the beginning of your LEGO Serious Play adventures. It was a practical guide to get you started. You now know enough to run the LSP sessions you need.

But like any skill, there are always improvements to be made.

The first step to improve your LEGO Serious Play facilitation skills is to do it. Run sessions. See what works for you, and work on the things that fall short. Experience is a great teacher.

After that, there are two options:

- **Courses.** There are a range of in-person and online courses you can take to further your skills.

- **LSP Community**. I started a community at *www.lspmethod.com* where you can improve your skills. It's a place to ask questions; read session reports; find articles, videos and podcasts; dive into the question library; and meet a friendly group of passionate people pushing the method forward. No matter where you learned LSP (from this book, a course or someone else) you are welcome to come and improve your skills.

You've taken the first steps by reading this book and testing the method. Experience, courses and community will take you even further.

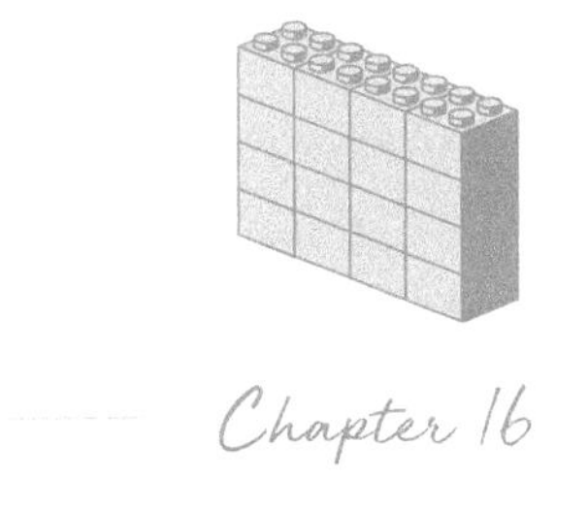

Chapter 16

CONCLUSION

My partner's brothers weren't that far off the mark when they accused me of being a drug dealer all those years ago.

I do deal in an addictive, mind-altering thing that is taboo.

LEGO Serious Play is like a drug: once you start doing it, you want to do more (and wonder how you lived life beforehand). It does change your thinking and relationships (in a good way!). And it is seen by the majority of corporate people as taboo (LEGO at work?!).

Even seven years later, my partner's brothers still wonder if what I do is real. They don't think I'm a drug dealer anymore, but it still sounds ridiculous to them.

Despite countless conversations, it's time I get them all in a room and run a LEGO Serious Play session with them, get them to experience it and finally put their doubts to rest. You'll always come up against doubts and scepticism. But by now you've read this book and tried it for yourself. You've seen what LEGO Serious Play can do.

As you do it more and more, you'll start to get this growing inner confidence about LSP. It works, and it works every time.

16.1 WHAT YOU LEARNT IN THIS BOOK

Let's do a quick recap of all you've learnt reading this book.

In chapter 1 you saw the problems we face when we gather in groups. By adding in LSP we change the process to change the outcome. This allows everyone to bring all their talents to the conversation.

In chapter 2 you learnt about the history of LEGO Serious Play and what a typical session looks like.

In chapter 3 you met a group of people who were just like you not that long ago. They learnt LSP and are now using it out in the world.

In chapter 4 you learnt when to use LSP and how to set up the room for a session, including what LEGO to use.

In chapter 5 you learnt the introduction to use for your LSP sessions.

In chapter 6 you learnt about Skills Building and how to warm up the group, as well as the four steps (Question, Build, Share, Capture) and two tips (don't have a meeting with yourself, story and metaphor). I also covered the all-important 'build a tower with you in it' activity.

In chapter 7 you learnt about the key activity of Individual Model building and how it forms the foundation of all LSP sessions.

In chapter 8 you learnt how to bring those Individual Models together into a Shared Model and some tips on how to facilitate it.

In chapter 9 you learnt about the Landscape activity where you move Individual Models around and show relationships using space.

In chapter 10 you learnt other activities: Shared + Landscape, Connections and Scenarios.

In chapter 11 you learnt a range of options for how to run the final activity, ensuring you take the great insights from your LSP session back into the real world.

In chapter 12 you learnt how to design your own customised LSP sessions including learning the thirty-minute-block design method, where to find your questions and what makes a great LSP question.

In chapter 13 you saw a range of example sessions.

In chapter 14 you learnt some of the important science behind the method.

In chapter 15 you learnt how to talk to people about LSP to get them into a session, as well as the trademark guidelines and how to take your LSP skills further.

16.2 OVER TO YOU

Wow, that is a lot in a small book.

So now you know. That's the LEGO Serious Play method.

But as I said, it's not the end. It's only the beginning.

You now have a new skill. Go use it. Get better at it. See what it can do for you.

And tell me how it goes. Send me an email at *michael@michaelfearne.com.*

I love hearing how people are using LEGO Serious Play to change the world.

Appendix 1

WHAT LEGO TO USE

There are four official LEGO Serious Play kits. Two are good. The other two I don't use.

- **LSP Starter Kit (2000414).** This is a great kit with a fantastic mix. It has 219 pieces.
- **Identity and Landscape Kit (2000430).** Another great kit. Much, much bigger (2,631 pieces). It includes DUPLO animals, lots of Minifigures and tools, basic bricks, baseplates and a lot more.
- **Connections Kit (2000431).** It costs a lot, has a lot of pieces and there is only one LSP activity you use it for (Connections). Skip this kit and either source connectors individually from LEGO or BrickLink or use other materials for the Connections activity (e.g., string, drawing).
- **Window Exploration Bag (2000409).** It's a small set with about forty pieces, but you have to buy it one hundred bags at a time. I don't use it.

CREATE TABLE KITS

When you want to run sessions with other people, I recommend putting together your own 'table kits', which are a special mix of several LEGO sets.

Each table kit has enough LEGO for six to eight people. I place the kit in a bag in the middle of the table. More tables? Have more table kits.

Here's how to put them together. There is a basic version, a fancy version and the 'I need lots of LEGO' version.

BASIC VERSION

Quantity	Style	Suggested Set
6	LEGO Serious Play	LEGO Serious Play Starter Kit (Set Number 2000414)
1	Bag	A play bag/mat (44 inch/110 cm), I use the Lay-n-Go cinch play bag

Dump the bricks into a big pile in the bag, put it in the middle of the table and you're ready to go!

FANCY VERSION

Quantity	Style	Suggested Set
6	LEGO Serious Play	LEGO Serious Play Starter Kit (Set Number 2000414)

Quantity	Style	Suggested Set
1	DUPLO	Wild Animals Set by LEGO Education (Set Number 45012) (it has double what you need) or any DUPLO set that has animals
1	Basic bricks	Bricks, Bricks, Bricks (Set Number 10717) or Large Creative Brick Box (Set Number 10698)
1	Minifigures—generic	Community Minifigure Set (Set Number 45022) or Fairytale and Historic Minifigure Set (Set Number 9349)
1	Baseplate (for Shared Models)	32 x 32 Baseplate (Set Number 10700)
1	Bag	A play bag/mat (44 inch/110 cm), I use the Lay-n-Go cinch play bag

Put all those pieces into the play bag, put it in the middle of the table and you are ready to go! Keep the baseplate off to the side for Shared Models.

'I NEED LOTS OF LEGO' VERSION

If you are running big sessions and need four to six table kits, here is another option.

The LEGO Serious Play Identity and Landscape Kit (2000430) has all the DUPLO elements, basic bricks, Minifigures and baseplates you need.

Get one of the Identity and Landscape kits and break it into four, five or six even piles (however many table kits you want to create). Then add four of the LEGO Serious Play Starter Kits to each pile. And because I have an irrational fear of running out of LEGO, I also put in more basic bricks. Put each pile in a bag and you have four to six table kits.

For each table kit, you will need:

Quantity	Style	Suggested Set
4	LEGO Serious Play	LEGO Serious Play Starter Kit (Set Number 2000414)
1/5th	LEGO Serious Play	LEGO Serious Play Identity and Landscape Kit (Set Number 2000430)
1	Basic bricks (optional)	Large Creative Brick Box (Set Number 10698)
1	Bag	A play bag/mat (44 inch/110 cm), I use the Lay-n-Go cinch play bag

In the end, it doesn't make a huge difference what LEGO you use; choose whatever you can afford.

The official kits are great because they have a good mix of generic pieces that help with metaphor and storytelling. The only thing to avoid is themed LEGO: no Harry Potter, Star Wars or Ninjago. It influences the story too much!

Appendix 2

GOING ROGUE

I've changed parts of the LSP method to make it better. I want to share with you how LSP is traditionally taught and why I made these changes.

ROGUE ONE

The four steps of LEGO Serious Play that I use are (1) Question, (2) Build, (3) Share, (4) Capture.

Traditional LSP has these four steps: (1) Question, (2) Build, (3) Share, (4) Reflect.

The first three are the same; the last one is different.

When I ran the traditional four steps, I found that a lot of that reflection and insight flew out the window and was lost. I wanted an explicit step to force people to capture those wonderful insights from building and sharing.

I could have tacked on another step to the end and made it five steps. But what I did instead was roll that traditional fourth step (Reflect) into the third step (Share).

Reflection happens all the way through Step 3 anyway. People share their stories, and then questions are asked and reflection takes place. In my version, there is also a group reflection at the end of Step 3 where the group reflect as a whole on all the stories shared. Then the group are all primed to capture that in the new Step 4.

In the end, all of the steps from the traditional approach are included, but now we have a better ending to the cycle with an explicit Capture step.

ROGUE TWO

As you saw in chapter 6, I use one activity for Skills Building: 'build a tower with you in it'.

Traditional LEGO Serious Play uses three activities:

1. Build the tallest tower
2. Build an animal (from instructions) and relate it to something using metaphor
3. Build a nightmare CEO or Build your dream holiday

Both my way and the traditional way achieve the same outcome: make people comfortable with the bricks and get them to utilise metaphor and story in their building.

But here's why I don't like the traditional way:

- It takes longer (forty-five minutes versus thirty minutes).
- It introduces the concept of competition (tallest tower), which is not what LSP is about.
- It includes building from instructions, which I hate, because that is the way everyone thinks about LEGO. I don't want to reinforce that when I'm trying to get people to think metaphorically.

Over hundreds of sessions doing the Skills Building activities, I've found my version quicker and more effective.

ROGUE THREE

You often hear other LSP facilitators describe Step 1 as Challenge instead of Question, as in 'I'm setting you a building challenge'. Even the *LEGO Serious Play Open-Source* guide calls it that.

But a 'challenge' sets up a potential for success or failure. In LSP, there shouldn't be that potential. No one should fail at LSP. The language you use in your workshop is important. You're asking questions, enquiring and exploring, not setting challenges.

These three changes have been tested over numerous sessions, and they make the LSP method better. It's nice to be aware of the old way, but my recommendation is to go with this new and improved way.

Appendix 3

HIGH LEVEL SUMMARY

Chapter 4: Pre-Session

- Is LSP the right tool?
- Design the session
- Set up the room

Chapter 5: Session Introduction

- What is LSP?
- Who uses LSP and why?
- Six bricks activity
- Why LSP is different from LEGO
- Objective of the session

Chapter 6: Skills Building

- Define the four steps (Question, Build, Share, Capture)
- Share the two tips (including examples)
- 'Build a tower with you in it' activity

- Explain This! activity (for groups that have already done the tower)

Chapter 7: Individual Models

- Individuals build LEGO models as answers to a question
- Your role as facilitator in each step

Chapter 8: Shared Models

- A group combine Individual Models into one Shared Model
- Your role as facilitator in each step

Chapter 9: Landscape Models

- A group keep their Individual Models intact and place them in the Landscape to show relationships
- Your role as facilitator in each step

Chapter 10: Other Activities

- Shared + Landscape (including Agents)
- Connections
- Non-LEGO activities

Chapter 11: Final Activity

- What do you normally do?
- Finish with actions: ORID
- Finish with something tangible: LEGO model or Kanban board

Chapter 12: Design

- Find your key questions
- Draft the session outline
- Refine the questions
- Where to use the power of LSP

Appendix 4

DETAILED CHAPTER SUMMARIES

CHAPTER 4: PRE-SESSION

The key to a successful LSP session is the work you do before the session. Using LSP in the right context, getting the design right and setting up the room properly.

4.1—IS LSP THE RIGHT TOOL?

LSP works well when:

- The topic is complex
- There is no one right answer
- You want everyone's input and engagement

LSP doesn't work so well when:

- The topic is very simple
- There is one right answer
- You want to keep control
- You're training people in a specific skill

- You've got the answer already and just want to 'transmit' it
- You want to physically, literally prototype something
- You have a very dysfunctional team
- You just want a fun team-building activity

4.3—DESIGN THE SESSION

Check out chapter 12 for more details.

4.4—SET UP THE ROOM

- Five to six people per table
- Big pile of LEGO in front of participants
- Tools to capture insights
- Slides and music at the ready

CHAPTER 5: SESSION INTRODUCTION

This is the five-minute introduction you do when introducing people to LEGO Serious Play for the first time. If they already know LSP, skip this introduction.

5.1—WHAT IS LSP?

- What LSP is: a method to help us think and communicate differently
- Where it came from: the LEGO Group in the late 1990s looking for a new way to do strategy

5.2—WHO USES LSP AND WHY?

- Highlight other companies that have used it
- Highlight the different uses: innovation, change management, strategy, customer experience, etc.

5.3—SIX BRICKS ACTIVITY

Run the six bricks activity in which each person finds six bricks, puts them together and tries to guess the number of combinations (915,103,765).

5.4—WHY LSP IS DIFFERENT FROM LEGO

Shift people's view from LEGO for building literal objects from the 'outside' world (e.g., cars, houses, castles) to LEGO Serious Play for building ideas and experiences from inside their minds.

5.5—OBJECTIVE OF THE SESSION

Remind people of the objective for the session and that LEGO Serious Play is simply the method you will use.

CHAPTER 6: SKILLS BUILDING

This is the twenty-five-minute block where you introduce people to the method and get them to practise it. You can't skip it; you can't shorten it. Running it like this ensures that you'll get better results when you get to the real questions.

6.2—THE FOUR STEPS OF LEGO SERIOUS PLAY

Outline what is involved in each of the four steps:

- Question. Facilitator asks a question.
- Build. Individuals build their answer to the question.
- Share. Each person shares the story of their model and others ask questions.
- Capture. Write down insights on cards and take photos of models.

6.3—TIPS

Outline the two tips:

- 'Don't have a meeting with yourself'
- 'Think in metaphor and story'. Give examples like the fear brick, the grass and your own tower.

6.4—ACTIVITY: 'BUILD A TOWER WITH YOU IN IT'

- Take the group through the 'build a tower with you in it' activity.
- Build. The group have three minutes to build. Give them time warnings.
- Share. Once the models are built, remind participants of the process for sharing: share the

story and ask questions. Everyone shares the story of their model.

- Capture. Get each person to capture insights on a card, then take a photo.

6.7—SECOND-TIME GROUPS

If you have a group already familiar with LSP, then you can do a quicker version of Skills Building that consists of:

- A quick reminder of the four steps and two tips
- Either the Explain This! activity or a random question to build as an Individual Model

CHAPTER 7: INDIVIDUAL MODELS

The Individual Model activity is the core activity of the LSP method. All the other activities are built upon Individual Models.

7.3—INDIVIDUAL MODEL STEPS

Question

- Deliver the question verbally and have it written up somewhere.
- Tell people how long they have to build.

Build

- Encourage people to get building; play music while they're building.
- Keep an eye out for anyone getting stuck (particularly if they're overthinking things).
- Give verbal time warnings halfway through, with one minute to go, with thirty seconds to go.
- Remember that these times are flexible.

Share

- One person shares the story of their model. Then open it up for questions from the group.
- Good questions are clarifying questions ('Does that brick have any meaning?') and probing questions ('Tell me more about...')
- Avoid 'why' questions
- Repeat for each person
- Group reflection at the end ('What did you all see and hear? Any themes? What were the key insights for you?')

Capture

- Decide beforehand how you want the group to capture insights: cards, photos, flip charts, whiteboards, videos.

- Collect photos in an online shared gallery like Padlet.

7.4—BUILD TIME

- Standard build time is five minutes.
- The range is two to eight minutes.
- Shorter times encourage more instinctive builds in which the model is usually about one thing.
- Longer times encourage more deliberate thinking and models with multiple aspects to them.
- Can do multiple shorter builds to get more ideas and models out.

7.5—BIGGER GROUPS

- Keep an eye across all tables during the Build step.
- Tables have to be more self-sufficient in running the Share step.
- Make sure all tables finish sharing at roughly the same time.

CHAPTER 8: SHARED MODELS

In the Shared Model activity, a group takes their Individual Models and puts them together to create one group model with one story.

8.2—SHARED MODEL STEPS

Question

- The group have gone through an Individual Model activity and have their models in front of them.
- Ask the question (remember that it's essentially the same question as the Individual Model activity, but it's about bringing those models together).
- Remind the group that they can pull models apart, and some parts of their model will be included and some will be left out.
- The meaning of the bricks must stay the same.
- Quick recap of each story by the participants.
- No time limit. Usually completed in thirty to forty minutes.

Build

- Step back and let the group form their Shared Model.
- If they get stuck, a good trick is to say, 'What do you like about someone else's model?'
- Three quarters of the way through, start to help the group refine the model: Devil's Advocate, Personas, Quiet Time, Move Around.

Share and Capture

- Get the group to practise the whole story through. It's a group storytelling effort; everyone has to jump in at some point.
- Get them to tell the story again as a group and record it on your phone.
- Reflect as a group: 'What did you see and hear? What were the key insights for you?'

CHAPTER 9: LANDSCAPE MODELS

The Landscape Model activity is when a group take their Individual Models, keep them intact and arrange them on the table to show relationships using space.

9.2—LANDSCAPE MODEL STEPS

Question

- The group have gone through an Individual Model activity and have their models in front of them.
- Remember that you can vary the number of models that each person builds in the Individual Model activity. Do you want them to build one, two or three models each?
- Ask the group to place their models in the Landscape and see what themes or stories emerge.

- Two rules: models remain intact and there needs to be some space between the models.
- Remind the group that where they place their models has meaning. How far from or close to other models they are, which way they face and how they are grouped are all important.
- No time limit. Usually completed in fifteen to thirty minutes.

Build

- Less building and more placing of LEGO models
- You, as facilitator, decide if this will be done as a freeform discussion or done in rounds
- Once the Landscape is formed, you can help the group to refine it with activities such as Devil's Advocate, Personas, Quiet Time, Move Around

Share and Capture

- Get the group to practise the whole story through. It's a group storytelling effort; everyone has to jump in at some point.
- Get them to tell the story again as a group and record it on your phone.
- Reflect as a group: 'What did you see and hear? What were the key insights for you?'

9.5—SHARED MODELS VERSUS LANDSCAPE MODELS

Shared Models

- Break up and recombine Individual Models
- Use a baseplate
- Total time: thirty to forty minutes

Landscape Models

- Models remain intact
- The table is the landscape
- Total time: fifteen to thirty minutes

Deciding between Shared versus Landscape

- If you want everyone to commit to one solution (e.g., strategy, a vision, team culture), do a Shared Model.
- If you have a range of answers and want to maintain their integrity (e.g., challenges, benefits, stakeholders), do a Landscape.
- If you are short on time, a Landscape is quicker.
- If you have a group that you think might struggle with compromise and consensus, do a Landscape.
- If you want to go deeper into a topic, do a Shared Model.

CHAPTER 10: OTHER ACTIVITIES

10.1—SHARED MODEL + LANDSCAPE MODEL

This activity is the layering of the three activities you already know: the Individual Model, the Shared Model and the Landscape Model. The aim is to build a Shared Model in the middle and then build a Landscape Model around the outside of it.

Steps

1. **Individual Models.** Run a standard Individual Model activity as described in chapter 7.
2. **Shared Model.** Run a standard Shared Model activity as described in chapter 8.
3. **Individual Models.** Run a standard Individual Model activity as described in chapter 7. Get each person to generate one to three quicker models.
4. **Landscape Model.** Run a standard Landscape Model activity as described in Chapter 9, except that you're getting the group to place their previously built Individual Models around the Shared Model in a Landscape.

The pattern to this activity is common understanding of a topic in the middle, and then a range of models around the outside. They could be Agents, challenges, risks, enablers, customers, solutions—anything, really!

10.2—CONNECTIONS

The Connections activity uses a physical LEGO connector to show relationships between models.

It's most commonly used after the Shared Model + Landscape Model activity but can be used to connect two models at any stage of a session.

Steps

1. Get the group to build some models beforehand. They could build two Individual Models each or a Landscape Model or a Shared Model + Landscape Model.
2. Lay out a range of LEGO connectors.
3. Get each person to choose a connector and connect two models.
4. After all the connectors have been placed, each person spends thirty seconds telling the group which connection they made and why.
5. For bigger, more complex models, repeat steps 3 and 4 to add more connections.

10.4—NON-LEGO ACTIVITIES

After building your LSP models, there are two options:

- Go straight to the final activity and crystallise those insights into action.
- Run some non-LEGO activities to dive even deeper and generate more insights.

Most of my sessions go straight to the final activity.

CHAPTER 11: FINAL ACTIVITY

The LSP method is so flexible and is used in such a wide variety of cases that there is no set way to end a session. The key thing to remember is that you can end a LEGO Serious Play session anyway you want!

But here are some ideas:

11.2—WHAT DO YOU NORMALLY DO?

Think of LSP not as an output but rather as a tool to help the processing of inputs. It's like a Post-it note or a whiteboard. There's no special output from a whiteboard. It's a tool that helps you visualise something with the end result being a better outcome.

Look to 'what you normally do' as a potential way to run your final activity and end your LSP sessions.

11.3—FINISH WITH ACTIONS

Use the ORID framework to develop actions the group can take:

- O: **Objective**. Ask the group, 'What did you see and hear?'
- R: **Reflective**. Ask the group, 'How did that make you feel?'
- I: **Interpretive**. Ask individuals to write down what their key insights were.
- D: **Decisional**. Ask individuals to write down what action they will take. Remind them to put down actions that they have control over: ones they don't need permission or extra resources to do.

11.4—FINISH WITH SOMETHING TANGIBLE

LEGO Model

- Get participants to build an Individual Model of the action that they will take. Going through the normal Question, Build, Share, Capture process.

Kanban Boards

- After the group have generated actions, get them to put those actions onto a Kanban board with three columns: To Do, Doing, Done.
- Have the board up in the work area where everyone can see it.
- Progress the actions along the board.
- Populate the To Do column with new actions.

CHAPTER 12: DESIGN

Your aim is to produce a customised session each time, moulded to fit your exact topic. Here are the steps to design your sessions:

- Find your key questions.
- Design your session outline.
- Refine your questions.

12.3—KEY QUESTIONS

Here are four ways I find my questions:

- Brainstorm the obvious questions.
- Ask your client what questions they want answered.
- Steal questions from other frameworks.
- Use questions from past sessions, including from the LSP community.

Remember that, at this stage, you're getting a feel for what your questions will be. Don't worry if they're not perfect.

12.4—SESSION OUTLINE

The easiest way I've found to outline a session is in thirty-minute blocks:

- Each block has one activity.
- The first block is always the intro and Skills Building. Tower for a first-time group. Quicker

Explain This! for a group that already know LSP.

- The second block is always an Individual Model.
- For the third block, I shift to group work (Shared Model or Landscape Model).
- Keep filling in blocks with activities and questions to achieve your objective.
- The last block is always the final activity that best fits your objective.

This thirty-minute-block design process can help you to outline any LSP session you want. But there are four outline patterns I've found particularly powerful:

- Individual -> Shared -> final activity
- Individual -> Landscape -> final activity
- Individual -> Shared -> Individual -> Landscape -> final activity
- Individual -> non-LSP content -> Individual

Topics and questions will change depending on the objective, but these patterns can cover a lot of sessions.

12.5—REFINE YOUR QUESTIONS

What makes a good LSP question? Here are some principles that help me to craft good questions:

- Low threshold, high ceiling (LTHC) questions
- Single focus, multi-part questions
- Positive/negative questions
- Past/present/future questions

- What and how questions
- Personal perspective questions

12.6—WHERE TO USE THE POWER OF LSP

Now that you know the LSP method and how to design sessions, the key choice is where to apply it.

- Use LSP at the start, the middle, or the end of a session?
- Use it at a high level or for diving deeper?
- For the whole session or only part of it, weaving in other techniques?

There's no one right answer. But as you start to think of your first sessions, think about where best to apply the power of LSP.

ABOUT THE AUTHOR

Michael Fearne is the founder of Pivotal Play, a leading facilitation consultancy that specialises in LEGO® Serious Play®. His clients include KPMG, Ernst & Young, Google and the innovation team at the LEGO Group.

He is also an expert at training people in the LEGO® Serious Play® Method. From consultants and coaches to academics and designers to facilitators and managers, he has trained hundreds of people to run their own sessions using LEGO® Serious Play®.

CPSIA information can be obtained
at www.ICGtesting.com
Printed in the USA
BVHW050843071221
623413BV00013B/678